The Art of Poetry volume 4

Love Through the Ages, pre-1900 poems

Published by Peripeteia Press Ltd.

First published September 2016

ISBN: 978-0-9930778-9-0

Peripeteia.webs.com

General Introduction to the The Art of Poetry series

The philosopher Nietzsche described his work as 'the greatest gift that [mankind] has ever been given'. The Elizabethan poet Edmund Spenser hoped his book *The Faerie Queene* would transform its readers into noblemen. In comparison, our aims for The Art of Poetry series of books are a little more modest. Fundamentally we aim to provide books that will be of maximum use to English students and their teachers. In our experience few students before A-level, and not all students at this level, read essays on poetry, yet, whatever specification they are studying, they have to write analytical essays on poetry. So, we've offering some models, written in a lively and accessible style. In Volume 1 we chose canonical poems for a number of reasons: Firstly they are simply great poems, well worth reading and studying; secondly we chose poems from across time so that they sketch in outline major developments in English poetry, from the Elizabethan period up until the present day. And, being canonical poems, they often crop up on GCSE and A-level specifications, so our material will be useful critical accompaniment and revision material. Volumes 2 & 3 focused on Forward's *Poems of the Decade* anthology, a set text for the Edexcel exam board. Volumes 4 & 5 explore the poems chosen by the AQA examination board for their *Love Through the Ages* anthology.

Introduction to *Volume 4: Love Through the Ages, pre-1900 poems*

The theme

According to the Bible it's the greatest of the virtues. According to 'The Beatles' it's all you need. According to Shakespeare it's like a summer's day or a star to navigate by, even during the roughest tempests. And it's also constant, altering not 'when it alteration finds'. Or it's a fever, a madness, a drug, a delirium. Music, apparently is the food of it. And it will always, 'Joy Division' tell us, 'tear us apart, again'.

A shape-shifter, it comes in many various types and guises: Forbidden and illicit; secret and intimate; spiritual and divine; brotherly and platonic; deathless or fatal; filial and patriotic; tender or tempestuous. The Ancient Greeks divided it into four types - *eros* [sexual passion], *agape* [unconditional and spiritual], *philia* [brotherly] and *storge* [empathy]. Surely it is the greatest, most written about subject of them all, greater even than death - love.

But, as the poet W. H. Auden asked 'What is the truth about love?' Does it reside, for instance, in the heart or the head? Is it a universal natural feeling or an abstract concept, malleable to time, place and taste? Is what we call 'love' the same emotion that Shakespeare and Donne and Wyatt felt and wrote about? Or has the idea of love changed? Is being in love to be touched by the divine, to be struck by a fatal disease? Or, perhaps, both? At the same time.

AQA's anthology of love poems might help us get a handle on the true nature of love. Herein we have the heat of love - lusty, seduction poems - as well as the agonies of love, love cooling and hardening into something bitter, or love unrequited, unfulfilled, love cruelly rejected. And illicit, secret or transgressive love is here too as well as fatal love, doomed love, love of parents and elegies for lost loves. In a handful of poems, AQA's anthology takes us through the antechambers of the human heart.

The company

A range of loves and also a range of tones, styles and voices. It's noticeable, and probably inevitable, that the Pre-1900 selection is dominated by male voices, all but one of these poets being men. But what a varied, colourful and voluble company of poets they are: Lords and commoners, Southerners and Northerners, Elizabethans and Victorians, novelist and dramatists, dreamers and realists. Imagine sitting them all around a large dinner table, providing some fine food and a few bottles of wine, or more, and then letting the conversation flow.

At the head of the table the elder statesman, Sir Tom Wyatt and Will Shakespeare, the latter watching and listening attentively with that sharp dramatist's instinct for great material. Nearby, the dark, sensual, handsome young John Donne is laughing at a witty quip by a sparkly-eyed, noble-looking, but rather wobbly on his pins, Lord Byron. Far more drunk even than Byron and considerably more foul-mouthed, the magnificently periwigged libertine John Wilmot is already slumped stupefied in his chair, only half-conscious of the hubbub that swirls around him.

Two fine, gallant looking, well-dressed chaps, Messrs. Marvell and Lovelace, are energetically vying for the attentions of the only lady present. Hair-tied back demurely in a bun, Christina Rossetti sips her wine and wears an implacable, perhaps amused expression, as the two men prattle on with their ever more extravagant and improbable boasts. Unused to such elevated, aristocratic company, the solid artisan figure of Will Blake is engaged in animated conversation with dapper Mr. Tom Hardy. As far as the somewhat melancholic looking, drowsy young cockney, John Keats, can make out their subject is visions and traditional song metres. Leaning in to join in is the hearty, ruddy-cheeked and convivial presence of the only Scot, Robbie Burns. At any moment this little group seems on the verge of breaking into impassioned singing.

Meanwhile, oblivious to it all, sitting quite alone, the dreamy thoughts of E. Dowson esquire revolve fixatedly on his absent love.

Quite a colourful crowd, we hope you'll agree.

*****

Why buy this book?

Search the internet and no doubt you'll find essays on most of the poems featured in the AQA anthology. Some of these essays will be good, perhaps great, while others will be moderate or poor or indifferent. Few, if any, however, will have been written expressly for A-level English Literature students and teachers following the AQA specification. Our essays are not designed to provide all the answers, or readings that can simply be learnt and regurgitated in exam conditions. Instead, we aim to demonstrate what happens when sharp critical analysis meets great literary texts. And, we try to express this analysis in a lively, engaging style, tailored specially for A-level students.

To engage in literary criticism is to enter a critical debate. When reading secondary material on a text you're not just looking for material to use, you should be searching for readings you agree with and, crucially, ones with which you disagree. Our essays are designed to inform and stimulate your own reading, to help you refine your own understanding, both of these poems and of what close reading of poetry entails. We hope and expect that sometimes you'll disagree with our interpretations; the experience will help you form your own alternative interpretations and have confidence in them. Our aim is to send you back to the poems with refreshed and renewed interest, so that you will read them more avidly and more expertly. In the end, that is the best way to get the most out of the experience of studying literary texts and of achieving the best results.

Critical methodology

In a recent article for the English & Media Centre blog[1] Barbara Bleiman worried about the quality of poetry criticism she was reading by A-level students who had entered their annual competition. In particular she opined that many students followed an over taught, rigid formula or checklist of features. Moreover, while students tended to do impressive and intricate close analysis they rarely related this to the ideas and effects of poems. In her words, 'many commented on small details without ever trying to come to an overall 'reading' of the poems, or trying to convey anything about what they found special or distinctive about that poet's writing in relation to others'.

Few students, it seems, understand poems as intricately working machines within which each part works in co-ordination with others. Rather than work through a pre-set formula, Ms Bleiman proposed a more open and flexible reading agenda for poetry. As she rightly says, 'if they'd followed through on their instant reactions and trusted them more, they would have been much more likely to get to the heart of what was most interesting about their chosen poems'. The authors would very happily echo these sentiments and, we hope, the varied essays in this book demonstrate precisely this sort of responsive and flexible approach recommended by the English & Media Centre. Here is Barbara's 'agenda' for poetry teaching and teaching criticism in full:

Students should:

- Read poetry in a different way from prose, acknowledging what is unique about it as a literary form and enjoying the different kind of reading and critical thinking that this implies

---

[1] https://www.englishandmedia.co.uk/blog/why-are-students-struggling-to-write-well-about-poetry

- Have an authentic response to it that is based on what really strikes them – the things that leap out at them as being interesting, unusual or special, trusting their own responses rather than assuming that someone else automatically has a more authoritative view that they need to adopt
- Explore aspects of language and form in relation to the big picture of what the poet is trying to communicate, rather than as micro-analysis for its own sake
- Think about such issues as tone and have the confidence to make a judgment about whether a poem is serious and reflective, wittily playful, or sharply satirical, intensely emotional or highly philosophical
- Subject their interpretations to scrutiny, so that they can justify to themselves [and to others], the grounds for their views and ensure that their readings are plausible and convincing
- Write poetry themselves, to get under the skin of the genre and understand what it means to write in a poetic form or forms. This might include writing their own poetry, writing back to poems, textual transformations and other experiments with poetry to understand the choices poets have open to them
- Read adult critical writing about poetry, to develop a sense of the kind of thinking they do and the unique ways in which they engage critically with this particular literary genre
- Read widely, beyond the confines of examination specifications, to develop confidence, familiarity and pleasure in poetry.

To us that seems like an excellent and wise agenda. And we hope this book provides exactly the sort of adult critical writing about poetry that will help to stimulate and refine your own individual responses.

 Our primary audience for this book is A-level students, but we've included teaching ideas that we hope might be of use to colleagues. [We've used the utterly unoriginal, but universally understood sign of the light bulb to signify a teaching idea. At the back of the book there's also a list of tried and tested revision activities which can be completed individually or with a class.]

AQA Love Poetry Through the Ages and assessment

Obviously we recommend that all teachers and students read the material on the AQA English Literature, specification A website to fully inform themselves about the nuances of assessment. However, what follows is a brief summary of key points and of particularly useful information.

All the exam boards have struggled somewhat with the new 'co-teachable' AS and A-level requirements. AS exams can now be taken as a stand-alone qualification at the end of the lower sixth or, alternatively, students can take an entirely linear A-level course and not be entered for AS levels at all. Some set texts appear both at AS and A-level and some only at one level. AQA A specification's Love Poetry anthology is, however, a set text at both AS and A level. But the assessments of this text vary significantly between AS and A-level.

At AS level students have to answer one question in their exams on one poem from the anthology. This question will ask them to 'examine' a particular critical view on a specific poem which will be printed on the exam paper. AQA has provided the following sample question:

'Examine the view that the speaker in *The Scrutiny* has a selfish attitude to love.'

Although there are slight variations on the weightings of each a.o.[2], for all English Literature specifications the assessment objectives are the same:

---

[2]For instance OCR have weightings of 30, 30, 20, 10, 10, putting more emphasis on close analysis and a little less on contexts.

AO1: Articulate informed, personal and creative responses to literary texts, using associated concepts and terminology, and coherent, accurate written expression. [28%]

AO2: Analyse ways in which meanings are shaped in literary texts. [24%]

AO3: Demonstrate understanding of the significance and influence of the contexts in which literary texts are written and received. [24%]

AO4: Explore connections across literary texts. [12%]

AO5: Explore literary texts informed by different interpretations. [12%]

Clearly the first three in this list are the most significant assessment objectives and this is reflected in the specific mark scheme of the poetry exam question. Here the 25 marks available are distributed as follows: AO1: 7, AO2: 6, AO3: 6, AO4: 3, AO5: 3. In short, a strong answer will be well informed, well written, perceptive, analytical and alert to the significance of contexts.

In their mark scheme for poetry AQA give their examiners the following useful prompts to aid marking:

• has the candidate engaged in a relevant debate or constructed a relevant argument?
• has the candidate referred to different parts of the text to support their views?
• has the candidate seen the significance of the text in relation to the central historicist literary concept?
• has the candidate referred to authorial method?
• the candidate's AO1 competence.

AQA's notes on AO3 also provide guidance for teachers and students in terms of narrowing and focusing the potentially huge area of 'contexts':

AO3: In exploring this poem about love, students will address the central issue of how literary representations of love can reflect different social, cultural and historical aspects of the respective different time periods in which they were written.

At A-level students will tackle an unseen task on poetry as well as a comparative essay. Both of these questions will be marked out of 25. The unseen task will feature two poems on the theme of love which students will have to compare. The second poetry question will ask students to compare at least two poems from the anthology with a novel from the list of set texts. The sample question AQA have provided is: 'Compare how the authors of two texts you have studied present barriers to love'.

Rather surprisingly, considering the comparative nature of both these questions, the weighting of the assessment objectives is the same as for the AS exam.

Applying this information to the essays in this book, we have aimed to provide well written and well informed close readings of each poem. Our main focus has been on close analysis of various aspects, such as imagery and form, but often this is informed by significant contexts, literary or historical. For each poem we also suggest others with which it could be productively compared.

Tackling the unseen

If Literature is a jungle, of all the beasts that roam or lurk among its foliage, from the enormous, lumbering Victorian state-of-the-nation novel to the carnivorous revenge tragedy, the most dangerous by far is a small, fast-moving beast, a beast untethered by place or time, a beast that is, in fact invisible. This infamous critter is called, simply, 'the unseen'. If that's sounds all rather alarming, let's bring the rhetoric down a notch or ten. How should you go about analysing an unseen poem and how can you prepare for this demanding task? In this case, by 'unseen' we don't mean a poem without any words, but a text you see for the first time in the examination hall.

To start with, we need to reiterate the fact that we don't believe there's one universally right method or blueprint for reading poems. If there were, all the varied types of literary theorists - Feminist, Marxist, postcolonial and so forth– would have to adopt the same working methods. Like the children depicted **above**, critics and theorists do not, in fact, all read in the same way. So, it's vital to appreciate that there's no single master key that will unlock all poems. A uniformly applicable method of reading a poem, or of writing about it in an examination, or for coursework, is like the philosopher's stone; it just does not exist. There's no 'Masonic password' or magic key that will give you instant access to the locked inner chamber of a poem's most secret meanings.

Having a singular method also makes the foolish assumption that all poems can be analysed in exactly the same way. A mathematician who thinks all maths problems can be solved with one method probably won't get very far, we expect. Instead, as Barbara Bleiman suggests, you need to be flexible. Trust your own trained reading skills. Respond to the key features of the text that is in front of you as you see them. It's no good thinking you will always write your second paragraph on figurative imagery, for instance, because what are you going to do when confronted with a poem entirely devoid of this feature? Although all the essays in this book explore fundamental aspects of poetry, such as language, form, themes, effects and so forth, we haven't approached these aspects in a rigid, uniform or mechanical way. Rather our essays are shaped by what we found most striking about each poem. For some poems this may be the use the poet has made of form. This is likely to be the case if, for instance, the poet has used a traditional or complex form, such as a villanelle. For other poems the striking thing might be imagery; for others still it might be the way the poet orchestrates language to bring out its musical properties.

In terms of critical approach, we champion well-informed individual freedom above over-regulated and imposed conformity. Hence, we hope our essays will be varied and interesting and a little bit unpredictable, a bit like the poems themselves. And we trust that if you write astutely and authentically about how a poet's techniques contribute to the exploration of themes and generation of effects, you really won't be going far wrong. [If you're interested in trying different methods of analysing poems, there is a concise guide in our A-level companion book, *The Art of Writing English Literature essays, for A-level and Beyond*].

So to reiterate: Always keep to the fore of your essay the significance and impact of the material you're analysing. Very sophisticated analysis involves exploring how different aspects of the poem work in consort to generate effects. As a painter uses shapes, brush strokes, colours and so forth, or a composer uses chords, notes and time signatures, so a poet has a range of poetic devices at his or her disposal. Try to relate the micro-details to the poem's 'big picture'.

 Think of a poem as a machine built to remember itself. Your task is to take apart the poem's precision engineering - the various cogs, gears and wheels that make the poem go - and to examine carefully how they operate. If you can explore how they combine together to generate the poem's ideas and feelings you will, without a shadow of a doubt, achieve top marks.

We believe your essays must express your own thoughts and feelings, informed by the discipline of literary study and by discussion with your teachers and peers. And, that your essays should be expressed in your own emerging critical voice. Finding, refining and then trusting your own critical voice is part of the self-discovery that contributes to making English Literature such a rewarding subject to study at A-level.

The essays herein are designed to provide you with the maps and tools, the essential survival kit in fact to thrive in the jungle of literature, kit that will help you master this collection of poems and tame that tricky little critter, the unseen. In achieving this mastery, you should also achieve great grades in your exams.

Writing comparative essays

The following is adapted from our discussion of this topic in *The Art of Writing English Literature Essays* course companion book, and is a briefer version, tailored to the AQA A-level examination task. Fundamentally comparative essays want you to display not only your ability to intelligently talk about literary texts, but also your ability to make meaningful connections between them. The first starting point is your topic. This must be broad enough to allow substantial thematic overlapping of the texts. However, too little overlap and it will be difficult to connect the texts; too much overlap and your discussion will be lopsided and one-dimensional. In the case of the AQA exam, the board obviously determines the broad topic they want you to discuss, love. The exam question will ask you to focus on the methods used by the poets to explore a particular aspect of this theme. You will also be directed to write specifically on language and imagery as well as other poetic techniques. And, of course, you will also be required to compare poetry to a prose treatment of love.

A three-way comparison can be tricky and awkward to handle, so we suggest that in terms of structuring your essay you treat the two poems as equivalent to a single text [A] to be compared to the prose text [B].In the diagram over the page we've treated the two poems in this way as one text, text A, and the prose novel is text B. As well as the novel, you have to choose two companion poems. Selecting the right poems for interesting comparison with the novel is obviously very important. To think about this visually, you don't want Option A, over the page, [as there's not enough overlap] or Option B [two much overlap]. You want Option C. This option allows substantial common links to be built between your chosen texts where discussion arises from both fundamental similarities AND differences.

Option A: too many differences

Option B: too many similarities

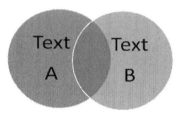

Option C: suitable number of similarities and differences

The final option will generate the most interesting discussion as it will allow substantial similarities to emerge as well as differences. <u>The best comparative essays actually find that what seemed like clear similarities become subtle differences and vice versa</u> while still managing to find rock solid similarities to build their foundations on.

How should you structure your comparative essay? Consider the following structures. Which one is best and why?

Essay Structure #1

1. Introduction
2. Main body paragraph #1 - Text A
3. Main body paragraph #2 - Text A
4. Main body paragraph #3 - Text B
5. Main body paragraph #4 - Text B
6. Conclusion

Essay Structure #2

1. Introduction
2. Main body paragraph #1 - Text A
3. Main body paragraph #2 - Text A
4. Main body paragraph #3 - Text B
5. Main body paragraph #4 - Text B
6. Comparison of main body paragraphs #1 & #3 - Text A + B
7. Comparison of main body paragraphs #2 & #4 - Text A + B
8. Conclusion

Essay Structure #3

1. Introduction
2. Main body paragraph #1 - Text A + B
3. Main body paragraph #2 - Text A + B
4. Main body paragraph #3 - Text A + B
5. Main body paragraph #4 - Text A+ B
6. Conclusion

We hope you will agree that 3 is the optimum option. Option 1 is the dreaded 'here is everything I know about text A, followed by everything I know by Text B' approach where the examiner has to work out what the connections are between the texts. This will score the lowest AO4 marks. Option 2 is better: There is some attempt to compare the two texts. However, it is a very inefficient way of comparing the two texts. For comparative essay writing the most important thing is to discuss both texts together. This is the most effective and efficient way of achieving your overall aim. Option 3 does this by comparing and contrasting the two texts under common umbrella headings. This naturally encourages comparison. Using comparative discourse markers, such as 'similarly', 'in contrast to', 'conversely' 'likewise' and 'however' also facilitates effective comparison.

When writing about each poem keep the bullet points in mind. Make sure you do not work chronologically through a poem, summarising the content of each stanza. Responses of this sort typically start with 'In the first stanza' and employ discourse markers of time rather than comparison, such as 'after', 'next', 'then' and so forth. Even if your reading is analytical rather than summative, your essay should not work through the poem from the opening to the ending. Instead, make sure you write about the ideas explored in the two poems and the novel, the feelings and effects generated and the techniques the writers utilise to achieve these.

Writing about language

Poems are paintings as well as windows; we look at them as well as through them. As you know, special attention should be paid to language in poetry because of all the literary art forms poetry, in particular, employs language in a precise, self-conscious and distinctive way. Ideally in poetry, every word should count. Analysis of language falls into a number of different categories:

- By 'diction' we mean the vocabulary used in a poem. A poem might be composed from the ordinary language of everyday speech or it might use elaborate, technical or elevated phrasing. Or both. Traditionally some words and types of words were considered inappropriate for the rarefied field of poetry. The great Irish poet, W. B. Yeats never referred to modern technology in his poetry - there are no cars, or tractors or telephones in his verses, because he did not consider such things fitting for poetry. When John Wilmot used the strongest swear words in his otherwise elegantly composed verse the effect was deeply shocking.

- Grammatically a poem may use complex or simple sentences [the key to which is the conjunctions]; it might employ a wash of adjectives and adverbs, or it may rely extensively on the bare force of nouns and verbs. Picking out and exploring words from specific grammatical classes has the merit of being both incisive and usually illuminating.

- Poets might mix together different types, conventions and registers of language, moving, for example, between formal and informal, spoken and written, modern and archaic, and so forth. Arranging the diction in the poem in terms of lexico-semantic fields, by register or by etymology, helps reveal underlying patterns of meaning.

- For almost all poems imagery is a crucial aspect of language. Broadly imagery is a synonym for description and can be broken down into two types, sensory and figurative. Sensory imagery means the words and phrases that appeal to our senses, to touch and taste, hearing, smell and sight.

Sensory imagery is evocative; it helps to take us into the world of the poem to share the experience being described. Figurative imagery, in particular, is always significant. As we have mentioned, not all poems rely on metaphors and similes; these devices are only part of a poet's box of tricks, but figurative language is always important when it occurs because it compresses multiple meanings into itself. To use a technical term figurative images are polysemic - they contain many meanings. Try writing out all the meanings contained in a metaphor in a more concise and economical way. Take for instance all the connotations packed into Romeo's famous metaphor comparing Juliet to 'the sun'. Even simple, everyday metaphors compress meaning. If we want to say our teacher is fierce and powerful and that we fear his or her wrath we can more concisely say our teacher is a dragon.

Writing about patterns of sound

What not to do: Tempting as it may be to spot sonic features of a poem and list these, don't do this. Avoid something along the lines of 'The poet uses alliteration  here and the rhyme scheme is ABABCDCDEFEFGG'. Sometimes, indeed, it may be tempting to set out the poem's whole rhyme scheme like this. Resist the temptation: This sort of identification of features is worth zero marks. Marks in exams are reserved for attempts to link techniques to meanings and to effects.

Probably many of us have been sitting in English lessons listening somewhat sceptically as our English teacher [dragon or not] explains the surprisingly specific significance of some seemingly random piece of alliteration in a poem. Something along the lines 'The double d sounds here reinforce a sense of invincible strength', or 'the harsh repetition of the 't' sounds suggests seething anger'. Through all of our minds at some point may have passed the idea that, in these instances, English teachers appear to be using some sort of Enigma-style secret symbolic decoding machine that reveals how particular patterns of sounds have such particular meanings.

And this sort of thing is not all nonsense. Originally deriving from an oral tradition, poems are, of course, written for the ear as much as for the eye, to be heard as much as read. A poem is a soundscape as much as it is a set of meanings. Sounds are, however, difficult to tie to very definite meanings and effects. By way of example, the old BBC Radiophonic workshop, which produced ambient sounds for radio and television programmes, used the same sounds in different contexts, knowing that the audience would perceive them in the appropriate way because of that context. Hence the sound of bacon sizzling, of an audience clapping and of feet walking over gravel were actually recordings of an identical sound. Listeners heard them differently because of the context. So, we may, indeed, be able to spot the repeated 's' sounds in a poem, but whether this creates a hissing sound, like a snake, or the gentle susurrations of the sea will depend on the context within the poem and within the ears of the reader. Whether a sound is soft and soothing or harsh and grating is also open to interpretation.

The idea of connecting these sounds to meanings or significance is also a productive 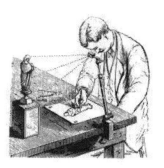 one. Your analysis will be most convincing if you use a number of pieces of evidence together. In other words, rather than try to pick out individual examples of sonic effects we recommend you explore the weave or pattern of sounds, the effects these generate and their contribution to feelings and ideas; the 'big picture' we've mentioned repeatedly. For example, this might mean examining how alliteration and assonance are used together to achieve a particular mimetic effect. An example will help demonstrate what we mean.

In *The Garden of Love* William Blake writes that priests are restricting his freedoms using the following image:

'Binding with briars my joys and desires'

A number of sonic devices are used here to mimic the sense of binding or knotting together:

- Alliteration of the 'b' is enhanced by the assonance of 'bi̲' and 'bri̲'
- Assonance stitches together the whole line: 'bi̲' – ''bri̲' – 'my̲' – 'si̲'
- Sibilance adds to the tight sound pattern; 'briars' – 'joys' – desires'
- Most of the poem employs cross-rhyme with rhymes in second and fourth lines of each quatrain. The switch here to internal rhyme brings the rhymes much closer together creating a mimetic sonic tightening.

Writing about form & structure

As you know, there are no marks for simply identifying textual features. This holds true for language, sounds and also for form. Consider instead the relationship between a poem's form and its content and effects. Form is not merely decorative or ornamental; a poem's meanings and effects are generated through the interplay of form and content. Broadly speaking the form can either work with or against a poem's content. Conventionally a sonnet, for instance, is about love, whereas a limerick is a comic form. A serious love poem in the form of a limerick would be unusual, as would a sonnet about an old man with a beard.

Sometimes poetic form can create an ironic backdrop to highlight an aspect of content. An example would be a formally elegant poem about something monstrous. Andrew Marvell, for example, employs the serious and elevated form of the Pindaric Ode for his elaborate chat-up spiel in *To His Coy Mistress*. Think of a thrash metal concert inside a church, a philosophical essay via text message, a fine crystal goblet filled with cherryade. These would be further examples of an ironic relationship between message and medium, content and context, meanings and form.

*****

Put a poem before your eyes. Start off taking a panoramic perspective: Think of the forest, not the trees. Perhaps mist over your eyes a bit. Don't even read the words, just look at the poem on the page, like at a painting. Is the poem slight, thin, fat, long, short? What is the relation of whiteness to blackness? Why might the poet have chosen this shape? Does it look regular or irregular?

A poem about a long winding river will probably look rather different from one about a small pebble, or should do. Unless form is being employed ironically. Think, for instance, about how Marvell uses form to generate a sense of time running out. Now read the poem a couple of times. First time, fast as you can, second time more slowly and carefully. How might the visual layout of the poem relate to what it seems to be about? Does this form support, or create a tension against, the content? Is the form one you can recognise, like a sonnet, or is it, perhaps, free verse? Usually the latter is obvious from irregularity of the stanzas and line lengths.

As Hurley and O'Neill explain in *Poetic Form: An Introduction*, like genre, form sets expectations: 'In choosing form, poets bring into play associations and expectations which they may then satisfy, modify or subvert'.[3] We've already suggested that if we see a poem is a sonnet or a limerick this recognition will set up expectations about the nature of the poem's content. The same thing works on a smaller level; once we have noticed that a poem's first stanza is a quatrain, we expect it to continue in this neat, orderly fashion. If the quatrain's rhyme scheme is xaxa, xbxb, in which only the second and fourth lines rhyme, we reasonably expect that the next stanza will be xcxc. So, if it isn't we need to consider why.

After taking in the big picture in terms of choice of form now zoom in: Explore the stanza form, lineation, punctuation, the enjambment and caesura. Single line stanzas draw attention to themselves. If they are end-stopped they can suggest isolation, separation. Couplets imply twoness. Stanzas of three lines are called tercets and feature in villanelles and terza rima. On the page, both these forms tend to look rather delicate, especially if separated from each other by the silence of white space. Often balanced through rhyme, quatrains look a bit more robust and sturdy. Cinquains are swollen quatrains in which the last line often seems to throw the stanza out of balance.

Focus in on specific examples and on points of transition. For instance, if a poem has four regular quatrains followed by a couplet examine the effect of this change. If we've been ticking along nicely in iambic metre and suddenly trip on a trochee, examine why. Consider regularity. Closed forms of poems, such as sonnets, are highly regular with set rhyme schemes, metre and number of lines. The opposite

---

[3] Hurley & O'Neill, *Poetic Form, An Introduction*, p.3

form is called 'open', the most extreme version of which is free verse. In free verse poems the poet dispenses with any set metre, rhyme scheme or recognisable traditional form. What stops this sort of poetry from being prose chopped up to look like verse? The care of the design on the page. Hence we need to focus here on lineation. Enjambment runs over lines and makes connections, caesura pauses a line and separates words. Lots of enjambment generates a sense of the language running away from the speaker. Lots of caesuras generate a halting, hesitant, choppy movement to lines. Opposites, these devices work in tandem and where they fall is always significant in a good poem.

Nice to metre…
A brief guide to metre and rhythm in poetry

Why express yourself in poetry? Why read words dressed up and expressed as a poem? What can you get from poetry that you can't from prose? There are many compelling answers to these questions. Here, though, we're going to concentrate on one aspect of the unique appeal of poetry – the structure of sound in poetry. Whatever our stage of education, we are all already sophisticated at detecting and using structured sound. Try reading the following sentences without any variation  whatsoever in how each sound is emphasised, and they will quickly lose what essential human characteristics they have. The sentences will sound robotic. So, in a sense, we won't be teaching anything new here. It's just that in poetry the structure of sound is unusually crafted and created. It becomes a key part of what a poem is.

We will introduce a few new key technical terms along the way, but the ideas are straightforward. Individual sounds [syllables] are either stressed [emphasised, sounding louder and longer] or unstressed. As well as clustering into words and sentences for meaning, these sounds [syllables] cluster into rhythmic groups or feet, producing the poem's metre, which is the characteristic way its rhythm works.

In some poems the rhythm is very regular and may even have a name, such as iambic pentameter. At the other extreme a poem may have no discernible regularity at all. As we have said, this is called free verse. It is vital to remember that the sound in a good poem is structured so that it combines effectively with the meanings.

For example, take a look at these two lines from Marvell's *To his Coy Mistress*:

'But at my back I alwaies hear
Times winged Chariot hurrying near:'

Forgetting the rhythms for a moment, Marvell is basically saying at this point 'Life is short, Time flies, and it's after us'. Now concentrate on the rhythm of his words.

- In the first line every other syllable is stressed: 'at', 'back', 'al', 'hear'
- Each syllable before these is unstressed 'But', 'my', 'I', 'aies'
- This is a regular beat or rhythm which we could write
  ti TUM / ti TUM / ti TUM / ti TUM , with the / separating the feet. ['Feet' is the technical term for metrical units of sound]
- This type of two beat metrical pattern is called iambic, and because there are four feet in the line, it is tetrameter. So this line is in 'iambic tetrameter'. [Tetra is Greek for four]
- Notice that 'my' and 'I' being unstressed diminishes the speaker, and we are already prepared for what is at his 'back', what he can 'hear' to be bigger than him, since these sounds are stressed
- On the next line, the iambic rhythm is immediately broken off, since the next line hits us with two consecutive stressed syllables straight off: 'Times' 'wing'. Because a pattern had been established, when it suddenly changes the reader feels it, the words feel crammed together more urgently, the beats of the rhythm are closer, some little parcels of time have gone missing.

A physical rhythmic sensation is created of time slipping away, running out. This subtle sensation is enhanced by the stress-unstress-unstress pattern of words that follow, 'chariot hurrying' [TUM-ti-ti, TUM-ti-ti]. So the hurrying sounds underscore the meaning of the words.

13 ways of looking at a poem

Though conceived as pre-reading exercises, most of these tasks work just as well for revision.

1. Mash them [1] – mix together lines from two or more poems. The students' task is to untangle the poems from each other.

2. Mash them [2] – the second time round make the task significantly harder. Rather than just mixing whole lines, mash the poems together more thoroughly, words, phrases, images and all, so that unmashing seems impossible. At first sight.

3. Dock the last stanza or few lines from a poem. The students' have to come up with their own endings for the poem. Compare with the poet's version. Or present the poem without its title. Can the students come up with a suitable one?

4. Break a poem into segments. Split the class into groups. Each group work in isolation on their segment and feedback on what they discover. Then their task is to fit the poem and their ideas about it together as a whole.

5. Give the class the first and last stanza of a poem. Their task is to provide the filling. They can choose to attempt the task at beginner level [in prose] or at world class level [in poetry].

6. Add superfluous words to a poem. Start off with obvious interventions, such as the interjection of blatantly alien, noticeable words. Try smuggling 'pineapple', 'bourbon' and 'haberdashers' into any of the poems and see if you can get it past the critical sensors.

7. Repeat the exercise – This time using much less extravagant words. Try to smuggle in a few intensifiers, such as 'really', 'very' and 'so'. Or extra adjectives.

8. Collapse the lineation in a poem and present it as continuous prose. The students' task is to put it back into verse. Discussing the various pros and cons or various possible arrangements – short lines, long lines, irregular lines - can be very productive. Pay particular attention to line breaks and the words that end them. After a whatever-time-you- deem-fit, give the class the pattern of the first stanza. They then have to decide how to arrange the next stanza. Drip feed the rest of the poem to them.

9. Find a way to present the shapes of each poem on the page without the words. The class should work through each poem, two minutes at a time, speculating on what the shape might tell us about the content of the poem. This exercise works especially well as a starter activity. We recommend you use two poems at a time, as the comparison helps students to recognise and appreciate different shapes.

10. Test the thesis that an astute reader can recognise poems by men from those written by women. Give the class *Remember* and *La Belle Dame Sans Merci* without the name of the poet. Ask them to identify whether the writer is male or female and to explain their reasons for identifying them as such. Try again with *Absent from Thee*. See what happens if you switch the gender of the pronouns in *The Flea*.

11. Split the class into groups. Each group should focus their analysis on a different feature of the poem. Start with the less obvious aspects: Group 1 should concentrate on enjambment and caesuras; group 2 on punctuation; group 3 on the metre and rhythm; group 4 on function words – conjunctions, articles, prepositions. 2-5 mins. only. Then swap focus, four times. Share findings.

12. In *Observations on Poetry*, Robert Graves wrote that 'rhymes properly used are the good servants whose presence at the dinner-table gives the guests a sense of opulent security; never awkward or over-clever, they hand the dishes silently and professionally. You can trust them not to interrupt the conversation or allow their personal disagreements to come to the notice of the guests; but some of them are getting very old for their work'. Explore the poets' use of rhyme in the light of Graves' comment. Are the rhymes ostentatiously original or old hat? Do they stick out of the poem or are they neatly tucked in? Are they dutiful servants of meaning or noisy disrupters of the peace?

13. Keats claimed that 'we hate poetry that has a palpable design upon us – and if we do not agree seems to put its hand its breeches pock'. Apply his comment to this selection of poems. Do any seem to have a 'palpable design' on the reader? If so, how does the poem want us to respond?

My love is as a fever, longing still
For that which longer nurseth the disease,
Feeding on that which doth preserve the ill,
The uncertain sickly appetite to please.

William Shakespeare, Sonnet 147

Sir Thomas Wyatt, *Whoso List to Hunt*

Fear and loathing in the Tudor court

Main things Thomas Wyatt is known for now: very important contributions to English poetry, esp. introducing the sonnet form to England. Main things Thomas Wyatt was known for during his life: being an ambassador for Henry VIII / petitioning the Pope re. annulling Henry's first marriage / getting imprisoned a minimum of twice / having a [rumoured] affair with Anne Boleyn and then watching her get her head cut off. The poetry too, but not so much. No one printed a word of his poems until fifteen years after he died, when Richard Tottel printed 97 of them in the runaway success, 'Songes and Sonnettes', a.k.a., 'Tottel's Miscellany'. So in the absence of any royalty cheques, with poems circulating exclusively around small networks of readers in letters or manuscripts, Wyatt made his living as a professional politician, a courtier, an attendant on the King whose demands he fulfilled, we can infer from the poems, with a mixture of loyalty and resentment.

For the court of Henry VIII was not a cheerful, open place, but a place of secrecy, betrayal, scheming and fear. Free expression was generally only encouraged in so far as it coincided with the opinions of the King, and the opinions of the King were liable to change quickly and without warning [see: Catherine of Aragon, Anne Boleyn, Jane Seymour, Anne of Cleves, Catherine Howard]. Wyatt was twice sent to the Tower on dubious charges of treason, and saw several friends go the same way as Anne [viz. beheading], and this heavy atmosphere of suspicion and duplicity informed not only the way he conducted himself at court, but also his poetry. Wyatt's verses, as such, are complex weavings of personal revelation and poetic concealment, unspeakable confessions masked in metrics, and none seem more dangerous than **Whoso List to Hunt**.

The poem is a reworking of Rime 190, *Una candida cerva*, by the Italian sonnet-master Petrarch, who was a Renaissance poet, one of the founders of Humanism, and who formed the basis for modern Italian literature, along with Boccaccio and Dante. The Petrarchan sonnet, which bears his name, is a strict poetic form of 14 lines, divided into an octave [eight lines] and a sestet [six]. In Petrarch's Rime 190, a white and golden-horned doe appears to the speaker at the confluence of two rivers, inspiring him to 'leave every task' and follow it, just as the twelve apostles did with Jesus. It is one of many translations of Petrarch's sonnets which Wyatt composed, but, as is the case with most of them, and especially with *Whoso List to Hunt*, 'translation' is less the word than 'transformation', since his poems differ so dramatically [in language and tone and even narrative] from Petrarch's originals. The dominant feeling of *Whoso List...*, for example, is less the ecstatic wonder of Rime 190 than bitter defeat: Wyatt's speaker has long pursued the 'hind' and, though 'wearied' of 'mind' and body, 'Fainting' as he follows, finds that he is still one 'of them that farthest cometh behind'. It has been a waste of time and energy, a 'vain travail', and, resigning the chase, he solicits any who may 'list to hunt' to do so, for he has the strength 'no more'.

The sonnet's first eight lines, its octet, bear almost no resemblance to those **of Una candida cerva**, but the connection between the poems becomes more obvious in the sestet, the final six, where Wyatt adopts Petrarch's unmistakable symbol of the collar, 'graven with diamonds', around the deer's 'fair neck'. But even here Wyatt conspires to deviate from his model: though the legend on both collars begins, 'Do not touch me' [with Wyatt's in the Latin, *Noli me tangere*], T.W. scraps Petrarch's 'It has pleased my Caesar to make me free' in favour of the far more sinister 'for Caesar's I am'. It's the possessive and threatening tone of these words + the knowledge of Henry VIII's sexual acquisitiveness and jealousy + the fact that hunting was such a common metaphor for courtly courtship + Wyatt's rumoured romantic affection for Anne Boleyn that has led many to conclude that *Whoso List to Hunt* is a cloaked confession of the poet's frustrated attempts to woo the object of the King's affection [or, at least, lust]. For Henry was England's 'Caesar'. And any woman to whom he laid claim was no longer, to extend the hunting metaphor, fair game.

Femme fatale

Those metaphors of hunting for a courtier's pursuit of a woman inevitably ascribe some pretty menacing and vicious connotations to the courtship. The women are, of course, dehumanised – sub-humanised – expected to 'flee' [as Wyatt's hind does] to make the matter interesting, but then willingly to submit once caught. The undertaking is more about acquisition than love, and the victim is therefore, as in hunting, ideally attractive so as to make more worthy a prize. But the metaphor ends at the moment of the 'capture': clearly the pursuer won't kill the pursued; the conquest will instead be sexual. And at various points in the poem, Wyatt seems to endorse this imagery of carnal conquest, making some fairly subtle but still savage references to the pursued woman's sexual integrity [or lack of it] in an attempt, perhaps, to ease his own frustration.

The very first line, for example – 'Whoso list to hunt, I know where is an hind' – suggests a], in the use of 'Whoso' or 'Whoever', that the woman will welcome pretty much any pursuer, and b], in 'I know where is an hind', that this is quite unlike Petrarch's sacred doe which vanishes as suddenly as it appears; this woman is easy to find and readily available. Then, further on, Wyatt keeps Petrarch's 'diamonds' around the deer's 'fair neck' but discards the topaz, which may seem insignificant, except that topaz was the stone of chastity. And then there's the clause, 'Who list her hunt', which begins the sestet, the sonnet's second part, providing a near-echo of the poem's first words in a demonstration of the sonnet form's capacity to contain both harmony and disjunction. But it is an uneasy clause, more urgent without the extra syllable of 'Whoso list to hunt', oddly configured in a Latinate syntax which positions the main verb, 'hunt', after the object, 'her'. And there's a suspicion that this unusual syntax is intended to invite the interpretation that

'hunt' isn't just the main verb, but also a pun on the vagina-synonym with which it rhymes, the oldest and most Anglo-Saxon obscenity of them all, the word which English poets from Chaucer onwards have loved to conceal in puns and wordplay.

And yet, despite the camouflaged vulgarity and the undeniable sexual aggression of the chosen conceit, there are many indications that the speaker relates to the plight of the deer – of, by implication, Anne Boleyn. The harassed 'hind' and his 'wearied mind' are allied by the rhyme scheme. The 'vain travail' of the pursuit is recognised, perhaps, as vain in the sense of 'vanity', as opposed to just 'in vain'. The 'Fainting' as he follows may signify a loss of conviction in the validity of the hunt, rather than merely losing strength. There is even the suggestion that the speaker identifies with the deer to the point of beginning to become her, and not just because the rime riche of 'hind' and 'behind' suggests that the pun on 'be hind' might not be an accident. He says, for example, 'Yet may I by no means my wearied mind / Draw from the deer', as if his consciousness and the fleeing doe have become inseparable, as if he is unable to distinguish his 'mind' – which can also mean 'sentiments' or 'opinions' or 'experiences' – from hers. And the apparent obstacle of their different genders is diminished by the fact that it was the white *stags* [the male deer, rather than the does] which wore the collars inscribed, *'Noli me tangere quia Caesaris sum'* ['Do not touch me for I am Caesar's'], in 3ʳᵈ Century Italy, and provided the inspiration for the image.

Born to be wild

So it seems that the speaker – Wyatt, presumably – is sympathising with the particular suffering of the much-desired yet 'owned' [or, at least, controlled] courtly woman. Such a sentiment can be inferred from the penultimate line. The phrase, *'Noli me tangere'*, is a Biblical one, taken from the passage in which Mary Magdalene, having mistaken the resurrected Jesus for a gardener, finally recognises him, and is rebuffed with the words, 'Do not touch me, for I am not yet ascended'. The proximity of this conspicuous scriptural reference suggests that the next clause, 'for Caesar's I am', is intended to recall another: Jesus's response to the Pharisees: 'Render unto Caesar the things which are Caesar's; and unto God the things which are God's'. That statement is made in reply to questioning about taxes and allegiance to an undesired ruler; it concerns money, wealth, and the idea of being owned. So it's spectral presence in the penultimate line of *Whoso List...* suggests that Wyatt was likewise reflecting on his relationship with his ruler, the role which money played in that relationship, and the extent to which, through the power of that financial bond, he had been bought and thereby 'tamed'.

He had, after all, been employed by the King for most of his life, having entered the service of the royal household as 'Sewer Extraordinary' [seriously] at the age of twelve. He held various positions over the following years, acting as an ambassador to the court of Charles V / the High Marshal of Calais / the Commissioner of the Peace in Essex / etc., but he was never off Henry's payroll for long, and must have felt pretty dependent on the monarch's grace. He was, in short, paid to be loyal to the King – even if patriotism or the fear of violent repercussions came into it, too – and would have been obliged to suppress any desires which would contravene the desires of his employer. Ideas such as continuing to pursue the woman who had already been claimed and similarly bought with the 'diamonds' around her 'fair neck'. [It's surely significant that 'hind' can mean not only 'female deer' but also 'domestic servant'.] So the royal subject and the royal object of affection would have found themselves in just the same predicament, and it's no surprise that the former began to relate to the suffering of the latter.

For it's one thing to suppress a desire, but it's quite another to extinguish it altogether. We can sense Wyatt really struggling with the task by the end of the octet, where he writes, 'I leave off therefore, / Sithens in a net I seek to hold the wind'. He's leaving off the hunt, he says; he's letting go of the yearning. A line like that should indicate the end of the poem, the conclusion of the thought, and yet Wyatt just can't force himself to give it up, and goes on making some further arguments and justifications to an individual, 'him', who feels like he might well be Wyatt himself, for another six lines. There's even the suggestion that being forced, or forcing someone, to suppress and snuff out one's / their desires is an interference in the natural order: 'Sithens in a net I seek to hold the wind' is a variation on an

Italian and English proverb which warns against seeking to control the uncontrollable, while the juxtaposition of 'I am' and 'I seem' in the final two lines stresses the conflict between the 'natural' wildness and enforced obedience of 'wild' / 'tame'.

With his break from Rome and the establishment of the independent English Church, Henry's reign was plagued by accusations that he was attempting to take control of that which he had no right to govern, that he was subverting the 'natural order' which placed God's supreme servant, the Pope, above any monarch. His desire to marry Anne Boleyn was, of course, the cause of the schism, and it's notable that Wyatt has one of his Biblical references in Latin and the other in English. But what's perhaps most significant about 'Noli me tangere, for Caesar's I am' and the line which follows it is that, though at first the 'I' seems undeniably to refer to the doe, a closer look calls that attribution into question. Certainly the words are round 'her fair neck', but that doesn't necessarily mean that they are hers. The passive voice of 'There is written' seems designed to make the matter uncertain. Are they the sentiments of the doe? Or her 'owner'? Or even Wyatt's? For Wyatt, we have seen, shares the hind's distress: he is a 'tame' courtier, but he's still an autonomous man with 'wild' desires of his own. He's a man who's been bought, but money alone can't quench our urges. And in *Whoso List to Hunt*, Wyatt takes his wild, unspeakable desires, the personal revelations he could never afford to make 'in letters plain', and half-conceals them, tames them, in a 'translation' of a much-admired poet's work, and in the sonnet's rigid form.

 'Crunching' a poem entails reducing each line to the single most important word. Obviously choosing this word is a matter of interpretation. A fruitful exercise is to crunch a poem individually in a class. Then, through comparison and discussion of the various options, to try to arrive at a class consensus or ultimate crunch. Further crunching can work towards reducing the poem to its single most important word.

The *Whoso List to Hunt* crunch:

HIND – VAIN – TRAVAIL – BEHIND – MIND – DRAW – FAINTING – WIND – HUNT – VAIN – GRAVEN – WRITTEN – CAESAR'S – WILD – TAME

Agree? Disagree? Why?

The focus on courtship links Wyatt's poem to *To his Coy Mistress* and *The Flea*. The sense of a love that is unattainable connects the poem to *She Walks in Beauty*. A number of other poems attest to the potential dangers of love, such as *La Belle Dame sans Merci*.

William Shakespeare, *Sonnet 116*

Type this sonnet into the great oracle named google and the following information is revealed:

Sonnet 116 is about love in its most ideal form. The poet praises the glories of lovers who have come to each other freely, and enter into a relationship based on trust and understanding. The first four lines reveal the poet's pleasure in love that is constant and strong, and will not 'alter when it alteration finds'.

Number one

Hence perhaps the popularity of this sonnet at weddings. In the pantheon of famous love poems, sonnet 116 most be close to number one. And with good reason.Firstly it's a sonnet, obviously, a form intimately linked with love. Its opening line declares true love as a platonic, intellectual ideal, 'a marriage of true minds'. It is a marriage because it is shared between two people - it is mutual, not lopsided or unbalanced. Love is also constant, true, never altering or warping or deforming into something else. Love is, of course, an abstract noun, but in Shakespeare's formulation it is so strong that it becomes almost a material object. And its physicality is robust, solid, stable, substantial; a source of strength it cannot be bent or shaken even by enormous pressure.

Even when its rejected, true love remains steadfast, it does not 'remove' itself. However rough life may get, whatever metaphorical 'tempests' we may face, love is definite and dependable -an 'ever-fixed mark' we can navigate with certainty by. Further metaphors for life's vicissitudes configure the individual as an imperilled boat ['wandering bark'] at sea, vulnerable to tides and bad weather.Love is a source of beauty and light, above us, a 'star' that guides us home, a little like the lighthouse in our illustration, only far better. In both of these cartographical images love gives us a sense of orientation, direction and security.

Conventionally sonnets follow a question/ answer, or call/ response form, with a hinge line falling between the opening octave and closing sestet. This hinge, or volta, signals the turn in the argument. Sonnet 116 rolls on after the octave without any turn, building a sense of onward momentum in one direction.Love, we learn, is not the plaything or servant of a capitalised Time. Physical beauty may be swept away by Time's grim reaper-like 'bending sickle' but love continues beyond the loss of good looks, 'even' to life's very end. And love is courageous, continuing constantly, loyally, selflessly 'even' to the rather onimously Mordor-sounding 'edge of doom'.

And, if you weren't convinced enough by that twelve line barrage of imagery, Shakespeare puts his reputation as a writer on the line. If he hasn't got this exactly right, then he never wrote a true word and, moreover, nobody in the history of the entire world has actually really been in love. Reverse engineer the statement: people have fallen in love, Shakespeare most certainly did write rather a lot, as the current example we're reading neatly illustrates, QED his definition of the nature of true love must be correct.

We can trust Shakespeare because he is at such pains to distinguish true love from something very close to it, something that might readily pass for love to a less astute and forensic observer. And he's also been puzzling over the nature of love during the previous 115 sonnets. The fact that true love and a counterfeit version, or some lesser emotion such as lust or infatuation, are hard to tell apart is emphasised by Shakespeare's word choices. Particularly significant are the sequence of paired words in the opening lines:

- Love / not love
- Alters / alteration
- Remover / remove

Such oppositions, of course, are food and drink to structuralist readers. For us the question is why didn't Shakespeare choose synonyms, such as 'changes' or 'leaver'?

The point, surely is the words are so similar to emphasise the fact that 'love' and its counterfeit, 'not love', are also very similar and hard to distinguish from each other.Just as each of these paired words share most of the same letters, so true and counterfeit love share many of the same features. Small, seemingly insignificant, changes to the words, such as adding just one extra letter, an 'r' to the end of 'remove', utterly changes the grammatical function of these words; so  minute differences differentiate true from counterfeit love. And these small variations actually lead to radical different, opposite actions. Such small differences, in other words, have enormous implications.

Let me/ let me not

So goes the case for reading *Sonnet 116* innocently as perhaps the ultimate attempt to define and celebrate true love in poetry. But there's another, more troubling reading that runs against this dominant interpretation. To start we might consider to whom the poem is addressed. In total Shakespeare wrote 154 sonnets in this sequence and he addresses a number of characters in the poems, including a handsome young nobleman who seems to be his patron, a 'dark lady' with whom he is also in love,as well as various rivals and enemies, both corporeal [another poet and admirer] and abstract [time, fancy, selfishness etc]. Scholars are not certain about the identity of these characters, though Henry Wriothesley, the dashing 3rd Earl of Southampton and Shakespeare's patron, pictured on the previous page, is the frontrunner as the young man. He certainly looks pretty sultry. In many of the sonnets Shakespeare worries about his own love being rejected by either or both the young man and the dark lady, who also seem to have a dalliance with each other - a classic love triangle. In sonnet 91, for example, after cataloguing all the young man's most excellent virtues Shakespeare concludes that he is 'wretched in this alone, that thou mayst take / All this away and me most wretched make'. Perhaps not his finest couplet, but the fear of rejection's palpable.

Scholarship tells us that the first 120 or so of the sonnets are addressed to the young nobleman and the last 25 or so to the 'dark lady'. <u>Doesn't the opening phrase 'let me not' suggest Shakespeare would actually rather like to 'admit' or introduce obstacles or impediments?</u>Perhaps the 'marriage of true minds' is not between Shakespeare and the poem's addressee; after all Shakespeare could not marry the Earl of Southampton. If that is the case then Shakespeare himself, as the rejected lover, might be seen as the impediment to the 'marriage'. This radically reverses the way we read the next lines. In fact their tone could now be read as accusatory, not celebratory.

In this reading, Shakespeare is distinguishing his true constant, unchanging love with the more fickle love of a lover who has altered and spurned him. The addressee, let's call him Henry, has removed and is wandering [to a different lover,

Shakespeare contemplating the 'edge of doom'/ a
reader contemplating a 'leap' of interpretation

perhaps the 'dark lady'] but Shakespeare heroically and selflessly and unrequitedly loves him still. And will not do anything now to get in the way of their relationship, he promises. Perhaps this explains that sudden exclamatory, emotional 'o, no!' Read in this way, all the celebratory and celebrated metaphors of love become coded and barbed, implying that Henry has fallen for a lesser, essentially counterfeit love. For example, the 'rosy lips and cheeks' do sound rather female as well as youthful, so Shakespeare would be insinuating that the love that has attracted Henry is superficial compared to his own timeless love. It also helps explain the otherwise overly ominous note sounded by the 'edge of doom'.

If, jilted, Shakespeare will have to love on from afar, removed from his beloved, this will feel like undertaking a journey to Mordor. Perhaps too, this subtextual, against the grain reading, might account for the oddly off notes generated by the sonnet's imperfect rhyming. Even accounting for changes in pronounciation over time, 'love / remove', 'come / doom' and 'proved/ love' seem unlikely to have ever harmonised fully.

Read this way, the poem is the equivalent of smiling through gritted teeth. Or a fist of steel in a velvet glove. Superficially it seems to be celebrating a couple's

41

relationship, but really it is making pointed comments. And, if we accept this, the poem itself becomes ironic: Shakespeare professes to not wanting to put any barriers up between the lovers; then he writes a poem that itself is a potent intervention and weighty impediment.

Convinced? Disagree? We'd have to read that opening line about 'true minds' as being pointed or sarcastic. Perhaps we're in danger of bending the lines to suit our interpretation. And aren't we making a huge assumption that the speaker in the poem is acutally Shakespeare and that the content is autobiographical? That seems to be a rather dangerous assumption for a poet more famous as a playwright. That said, even if we shed the autobiographical reading, the poem could still be addressed to a beloved by a character whose lover has been rejected. You'll have to decide. Or, as in the examination you'll be asked to argue for and against a critical proposition about one of these poems, perhaps you don't need to take a leap one way or another.

Maybe the opening of sonnet 117 might give us a clue: 'Accuse me thus: that I have scanted all/ Wherein I should your great deserts repay'. Hardly sounds like a joyous continuation of a celebration of true love, does it? But, then again, scholars argue over the correct sequence of the poems and, indeed, whether they even form a coherent sequence.

Let me not crunch

TRUE – IMPEDIMENTS – ALTERS – REMOVER – EVER-FIXED – NEVER – STAR – UNKNOWN – FOOL – SICKLE – LOVE – DOOM – ERROR – NEVER

As you'll discover, we're quite partial to finding coded meanings that run against the apparent overt sense in these poems. In this way, Sonnet 116 could be linked interestingly to *Whoso List to Hunt* and *Ae Fond Kiss*.

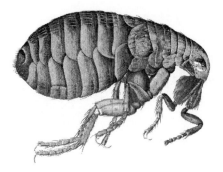

John Donne, *The Flea*

Imagine to your surprise/ delight/ horror you have been asked to write a new biography of the brilliant and revolutionary metaphysical poet John Donne. How might you start your first chaper? Perhaps it would handy to have a brief outline of Donne's life with which to work.

Born into a Catholic family in the late sixteenth century, Donne was a prodigously bright boy sent to Oxford University aged just twelve. Being a Catholic he could not, however, graduate, but this did not stop him progressing to Lincoln's Inn law school in London to train as a lawyer. During and after his time at studying Law, Donne seems to have led a rather rakish and profligate life. According to wikipedia, for instance, he 'spent much of his considerable inheritance on women, literature, pastimes and travels'. After law school Donne travelled to Spain and probably fought alongside the Earl of Essex and Sir Walter Raleigh in the battle of Cadiz. Things were, it appeared, going very well for the young, talented, ambitious John Donne. By 25 he had been appointed secretary to Sir Thomas Egerton, Lord Keeper of the Great Seal, the most senior lawyer in the land.

However, now things took a turn for the romantic. Donne fell in love with the aristocratic Anne More, Sir Thomas's ward. Despite the fact that, socially, she was completely out of his league and despite the fact that Donne had written racily about his many relationships with women, Anne and he became lovers and, without the consent of her parents,a few years later the couple were married in secret. As John Stubbs writes in *Donne the Reformed Soul*, the marriage was an incredibly bold and daring act: 'The lovers had defined themselves against every social and marital convention in the land'.[4]Unsurprisingly, upon discovery of the marriage Donne was sacked from his job. Worse, he was arrested and incarcerated in the Fleet prison. As the poet succinctly commented at the time, 'John Donne, Anne Donne, undone'.

It took years for Donne to haul his life and career back on track. But by 1615 he had renounced his Catholicism, converted and been ordained into the Church of England. And completing his ascent back up the slippery slope of English society, in 1621 he was made Dean of St. Pauls Cathedral, one of the most senior and distinguished posts in the Church of England.

So, back to the original question, how would you start your biography?

Here's how John Stubbs starts his book on Donne's life:

'His mistress lived with her parents, and access was a problem. Donne had to devise a way of walking that kept his silk suit from 'whistling' as he skulked through the creaky mansion. The family's grim, eight-foot-high, iron-bound serving man was always on the look out, and the lady of the house, who lay buried in her bed while the young couple shook the floor by night, looked carefully for signs of 'paleness, blushing, sighs and sweats' by day. The matron had her suspicions. She would take her daughter aside and try extracting a confession...' [5]

Pretty racy stuff, for a literary biography. And this is how we'd like you to think of John Donne, the archetypal clandestine lover, creeping silkily across a landing late at night, evading the guardians protecting a beautiful woman, to engage, we suspect, in an illicit relationship. This most certainly is the daring poet of ***The Flea***, a poem once described by an eminent [though rather prudish] literary critic as 'about

---

[4]John Stubbs, *Donne the Reformed Soul*, p. 155
[5]Ibid, p. 3.

the most merely disgusting in our language' [6] It is the poet who could tell his beloved in another rather forward poem, to undress and 'licence my roving hands, and let them go / Before, behind, between, above, below'.

In his book on Donne, John Carey opens very differently, but in a way no less significant to reading *The Flea*. Carey's first chapter is titled **Apostasy** and it begins:

'The first thing to remember about Donne is that he was a Catholic; the second, that he betrayed his Faith'. [7]

Keep this in mind when thinking about falsity and truth, loyalty and deceit, honour and shame in *The Flea*.

Fleas are, of course, disgusting little critters, disease-carrying irritants and parasites. In Donne's poem he suggests he is jealous of a flea and goes on to imagine the flea's body forming the lovers' 'marriage temple'. Clearly this is a preposterous metaphor. And that, of course, is the point. The wit of the poem lies in making the ridiculous comparison between the lovers and a flea sound convincing. For metaphysical poets wit was defined as 'discordia concors'; finding similarity in things apparently dissimilar -the more improbable the two things compared the greater the wit.

To give a class a flavour of this wittiness show them a series of paired images and ask them to come up with as many similarities as possible in a few minutes of brainstorming. First pair a love heart with a picture of a sunny summer's day. Secondly, pair a love heart and a red rose. Thirdly a flea and a church. If they get good at it, you could provide some further unlikely pairings that could form the base of a future poem. How, for example is an apple like an airplane, love like a classroom, modesty like a bowl of wholesome cereal?

---

[6] This is the judgement of Sir Arthur Quiller-Couch
[7] John Carey, *John Donne, Life, Mind and Art*, p.1

A silver tongue

Obviously Donne's is a carpe diem, seduction poem. The poet is trying to persuade a woman to go against her better judgement and her honour and all the weight of social mores and prohibitions of the period and her parents' wishes, to have sexual intercourse with him before marriage. Strip the poem of its elaborate, balanced, playful language, peel off its elegant structure and it's a chat-up with a very dodgy line of argument. Viz.:The flea has bitten both of them therefore their blood has 'mingled' inside the flea→Which means they have already had sexual intercourse, kind of, in a way ['Bloods mingled be' is an euphemism for sex] →Yet the woman, paradoxically, has not lost her virginity ['maidenhead'] despite having sex!→When the Lady expresses her disdain for this transparently specious argument in the second stanza, Donne has to take a new tack: →Inside the flea, as their blood is mixed, the would-be lovers are, in effect, already married. →Therefore the flea's interior is a 'marriage temple'→So, if the lady squashes the flea, and by extension flattens Donne's argument and snuffs out his lust, she destroys a temple, kills the charming poet and spills the blood of a poor innocent, i.e. the flea. Formidable sins in themselves, but, worse, she will also commit another sin, self-murder→Evidently the lady sees through this flimsy logic and squashes the flea. With only a few lines of the poem left, it seems as if Donne has been vanquished and his suit rejected. But, with characteristic quick wit the poet manages to use this turn of events to his advantage→'Aha!' quoth he, the fact that the lady has been [miraculously] unharmed by the death of the flea just goes to prove how fear can mislead us→QED she does not need to fear being seduced. Indeed she will not lose her honour because, well, because she was not harmed by the death of the flea, despite his argument that killing the flea she'd kill herself. Sounds water-tight and convincing to me, your honour.

Of course, Donne is not really trying to be convincing.
He knows that his argument doesn't really make sense. The poet's tongue is firmly in this cheek and the knowing, amusing self-mockery is also part of his seduction routine.

Power dynamics

The Flea is a dramatic poem. We are invited to imagine a scene where the poet, or a lusty character he's created, is addressing a virginal and proper young woman in some kind of private space where they can talk intimately. Perhaps Donne's has made it across the landing to the sacred bedchamber. It's a one-sided dialogue. The lady is given no words, which might suggest the male poet is very much in the boss seat. But, of course, silence can express power and, in the equivalent of stage directions, we discover that the lady acts decisively and dismissively. Actions, they say, speak louder than words. The action of moving to squash the flea retrospectively helps us to read her silence as at least sceptical, if not downright hostile to Donne's absurd argument. Imagine her listening, head cocked to one side, eyebrow raised, arms folded firmly across her chest. A withering look.

Having made the point that we should not necessarily equate the poem's speaker with Donne himself, for the sake of consistency I will refer to the speaker of the poem henceforth as Donne. Donne starts off in masterful, authorative vein:

'Mark but this flea, and mark in this...'

Two quick imperatives, expressed in simple, emphatic language. This is the language of instruction. The speaker is going to go on to use the flea to illustrate his point, speaking from on high, talkng down to his addressee, who perhaps is not very bright. For Donne has to spell things out in monosyllables. However, the imperious tone changes abruptly at the start of the second stanza:

'Oh stay, three lives in one flea spare...'

Magisterial imperatives are replaced by a shocked, pleading, excalamatory sentence. The balance of power tips violently and the speaker's toppled from his pedestal. Though he recovers his equilibrium somewhat he ends this stanza with 'let not...', a sure indication of where the power lies. Or so it appears. Two rhetorical questions open the last stanza, also signalling Donne's apparent loss of power:

'Cruel and sudden, hast thou since
Purpled thy nail, in blood of innocence?'

If we conceive of the scene as a contest, one between Donne's lusty and vigorous rhetoric and the lady's demure protective actions, at this point, so near the end of this battle of the sexes, the lady appears to have won, hands down. Donne's imagery encourages the analogy of a fight: The virtuous woman 'triumph'st' after killing the flea and moments later, the defeated speaker 'yield'st'. The switch between those two verbs signals, however, the sudden restoration of Donne's dominance of the scene. The tables have turned again. The certainty of '**when** thou yield'st' expresses supreme confidence in the poet's victory and in the last lines the imperative tone returns resoundingly, 'then learn how...' Here endeth his  lesson.

Critics often point out that in Shakespeare's plays the bard's choice of second person pronouns is significant, revealing underlying power dynamics between characters. Broadly the polite, formal, respectful term to use when addressing a personage of higher status was 'you'; 'thou' was employed when talking to those of lower status or in an intimate context. Like Shakespeare, Donne also moves tellingly between the two versions of the pronoun. In the first and last stanzas he consistently uses the more familiar 'thou' and 'thee', emphatically so in the last stanza where it's employed no less than six times in eight lines. In contrast 'you' is utilised exclusively in the second stanza. As with the tone, type of sentence and the imagery, these pronouns neatly reveal the shifting power dynamics of the poem's little courtship drama.

Enormous and disgusting hyperbole

Above are the words of the Augustan poet and dictionary writer Samuel Johnson passing judgement on Donne's poetry. Not a fan, evidently. Indeed critical opinion of Donne, and his fellow metaphysical poets, has divided on the issue of whether his/ their original metaphors and conceits are brilliantly imaginative or preposterously improbable. In *The Flea* Donne compares this little parasite to a man – a seducer who 'woos' a lady, a 'pampered', favoured lover who 'sucks' the blood of their beloved and later to a murder victim whose 'innocent' blood has been spilt - to a bed of procreation where 'bloods' are mingled as well as to a large sacred building, a 'temple' in which the lovers are 'cloistered' within its 'living walls of jet'. He also

contrasts the flea's swelling with his own lack of arousal. Think about this elaborate conceit for a moment and consider the picture of a flea above and you'll recognise Johnson's point. Certainly there's not much visual correspondence between a flea and a temple, for instance. There's something extraordinary too in

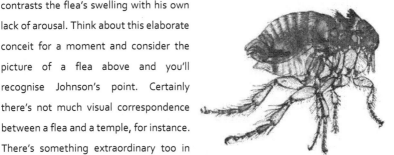

the way Donne's imagery scales up the microscopic flea to the point where it is some sort of church. But to condemn Donne for such an improbable or forced comparison would to miss the point and the humour of the poem. It would be to assume the poet did not know that his imagery was preposterous.

Being outrageous, daring, shocking and amusing was part of the seduction. It is part of his charm and attraction that he is a hot, young lover with no time for outmoded social conventions, impatient with social decorum, contemptuous of the rules laid down by crusty parents. He also has to scale his lady's own defences. However much it may frustrate the amorous lover, the pursued lady's defensiveness is understandable, especially given that her social respectability and future marriage prospects rest on her maintaining the 'maidenhead' he is so busily besieging. To this end, Donne uses the sort of highly suggestive, nudge-and-wink sexual imagery that would put a saucy seaside postcard to shame. Unsubtle it may be - the repeated use of the verb 'suck', the reference to intercourse, the swelling with blood - and outrageously cavalier, but that's hot, young lovers for you. Unsurprisingly, the older, wiser, highly respected Dean-of-St-Pauls Donne was embarrassed by the work of his earlier years. And it wasn't just the nudge-and-winkness and the two-finger salute to convention that would have made the old Dean squirm. Scandalously, young lover Donne employed religious language as just another tool of seduction, treating the sacrament of marriage with unconcealed rhetorical levity.

A dance of form

With its lusty language and monstrous hyperbole we might conclude that Sir Arthur Q-Crouch was correct in thinking *The Flea* a rather crude poem [the noble sir called it 'disgusting', you will recall]. The wry self-presentation might lighten the sauciness a little, but it's really in the form of the poem that its elegance resides. The form of

the stanzas and the rhyme scheme provide a counterbalancing regularity of grace and poise. In particular Donne plays around with the idea of twos [the two lovers] and threes [the lovers plus the flea]. The poem's form is like an elaborate dance of twos and threes. There are three even, regular stanzas. Each of these is composed of three couplets [two consecutive lines rhyming with each other] and each stanza ends with a triple rhyme, or triplet. Both a classic love triangle and a perverse trinity. It is also noticeable that all the rhymes are full masculine ones. The way they click neatly into place is like the sharp turn of a heel in a dance. It looks easy because the whole thing is accomplished with considerable panache.

Characteristically, however, within this external elegance and neat order Donne smuggles in some rebellion against smooth convention. If the poem is a formal dance, Donne has invented some new moves of his own. Conventionally Renaissance poems were written in single dominant metre, such as iambic pentameter. Donne flouts this artistic convention, just as he flouts conventions about sex and religion. His metrical pattern is rougher and looser than was conventional, as he wanted his verse to have the quality of impassioned speech. The sort of speech he might have made in a bedchamber having silenced his silk pantaloons and evaded the eight foot giant. Take just the first two lines by way of example:

'MARK but this **flea,** and **mark** in **this**
How **little that** which **thou** deniest **me** is'.

Starting with two strong stresses, from the first beats the metre is irregular. And it's a stressy, knotty line because 1. It has too few unstressed syllables and 2. It's entirely composed of monosyllables. The second line straightens out into a more regular iambic pentameter, but even here the syntax feels contorted, with the verb shoved to the end of the line and an uncertain stress pattern in the final feet. And so the poem proceeds. Disorder within order, rebellion within convention.

Donne shows a delight in paradox in *The Flea*, the idea that you could lose something and yet not lose it. Elsewhere in his poetry, particularly in his later religious poems, he explores paradox in more serious mode. The central paradox, of course, became the Christian one that we have to die to wake to eternal life. But even in his earlier love poems, we see Donne playing around with issues of truth and lies, loyalty and deceit, honour and shame, appearances and reality.

A crunched *Flea*

MARK – DENY'ST – SUCKS – MINGLED – CONFESS – SIN – ENJOYS – PAMPERED – ALAS – STAY – MARRIED – FLEA – BED – PARENTS –

CLOISTERED – KILL – MURDER – SACRILEGE – CRUEL – INNOCENCE – GUILTY – DROP–TRIUMPH'ST – WEAKER – LEARN – YIELD'ST – LIFE

The obvious comparison is to the other Carpe Diem seduction poem in the anthology, *To His Coy Mistress* which we explore next. The male predator female prey motif links it to *Whoso List to Hunt*, while Lovelace's *The Scrutiny* and Rochester's *Absent from Thee* also feature tendentious rhetoric employed for dubious ends. What distinguishes Donne's poem from the examples above is that the lady is granted agency and the poet mocks himself. Someone once said there are only two subjects in Donne's poerty, Donne and other things. You might bear this in mind when looking for poems for comparison.

Andrew Marvell, *To his Coy Mistress*

It is a truth universally acknowledged that in the most common of all stories [the boy meets girl story] it is the boy who must insist on getting it on. All the while the innocent, naïve and prudish girl must instigate a great strategy of joyless and moral defence. Or so Andrew Marvell [pictured] would have you believe. And who could argue with that face; with that thinly veiled sneer of contempt; with that beautifully manicured moustache? 'His Coy mistress' is the answer to that particular question. She is seemingly oblivious to his various arguments for indulging in sensual/sexual pleasures and has compelled him to vent his frustrations into poetic form instead. What an inconsiderate young wench!

'I'm so hot for her and she's so cold'

The poem is dominated by the male speaker, whose strong subjective persuasion finds its focus on the significant other in the poem: his 'coy mistress'. This crucial adjective tells us much about the relationship itself. The stereotypical active male is laying siege to the defences of the passive female, who fends off his advances through coyness. It epitomizes the age old struggle of seduction, where the wily female must preserve her honour while not alienating the male completely. Commonly associated with coquettish women, this coyness, when viewed from one end of the gender telescope may represent sexual frustration of the most infuriating kind, while viewed from the opposing end it's an essential weapon in ensuring social respectability.

What Marvell cleverly constructs is an oppositional pairing or binary opposite of man – woman; active – passive; subject – object; heat – cold; risk – caution; realistic – idealistic. It smacks of the classic persuasive battles that we would still recognize today but also tells us something about the gender norms of the 17th century. There is a distinct feeling of space and difference and even separation between the speaker and the mistress throughout the poem, especially in the gothic darkness of the second stanza. Conveniently, the logical endpoint of both the poem and the speaker's argument sees the two lovers become one [to utilize an overused pop cliché]. There is no longer a distinct sense of 'You and 'I'; instead it becomes a case of 'Us' and 'We'. The result of such clever transformation from twoness to oneness, from separation to togetherness, is unclear. We never know whether coy becomes joy. Like Marvell, the reader is made to wait as the sensual drama of the poem is never resolved.

To His Coy Mistress is a poem wracked by oppositions. The unity suggested by the 'we' of the first line is swiftly broken into a distinct 'I' and 'you'. Throughout the poem a whole series of oppositions emerges that would make structuralists the world over rejoice:

- I vs. you

- Male vs. Female

- Conquest vs. Defence

- Excess vs. Scarcity

- Indulgence vs. Denial

- Pleasure vs. Honour

- Spontaneity vs. Calculation

- Present vs. Future

- Realism vs. Idealism

- Hot vs. Cold

- Life vs. Death

Marvell also constructs another important opposition in the poem: between the speaker and a very abstract entity: Time. Time in various forms is the chassis of Marvell's vehicle for sensual indulgence. It is a vital weapon in the lascivious logic of

the speaker in trying to persuade his mistress to have sex with him. But Time changes shape, so to speak, as the poem progresses. Initially it is an inert thing; as abstract as it really is. However, upon charging into

the second stanza Time becomes personified as a heartless predator and thus Time becomes as much of an opponent as the speaker's mistress. In fact the end of the poem becomes more a battle with mortality and the speaker's awareness of the transience of youth and pleasure. In some ways, his apocalyptic persuasive trick of using the tomb has backfired. He has taken his eye off the ball, persuasively speaking, and becomes more obsessed with trying to defy the passage of Time rather than complete his sexual conquest.

The logic of love

The speaker in the poem is confident and strong, full of certainty in his addressing of his lover. The title indicates the poem's modus operandi: it is an appeal to or, maybe even an argument with, a reluctant lover. In the Restoration comedies that dominated the stage of Marvell's later life such male persuasion of guarded female lovers to submit to sensual appetites was rife. However, such antics are not just restricted to Restoration theatre; the battle of the sexes is a universal one. And to put it frankly, the fallout of such struggles remains universal: personal rejection or personal validation through enjoyment. In a time without the benefits of contraception and much more stringent social codes, the problem of illegitimacy was much greater than today. Hence, the struggle between carpe diem & family planning becomes much more violent!

The speaker certainly has a complaint to make: his mistress will not submit to his sexual advances. The poem presents a clever argument that is typical of the metaphysical poets of Marvell's time. The structure of the poem can be summarized succinctly as follows:

IF we had oodles of time →BUT we don't →SO it's loving time!

Clearly it seems a logical, if completely self-serving, structure. The structure of the poem is that of an amorous argument with hypothesis, anti-hypothesis and conclusion and results in a curious combination of rational logic and intimate seduction. Repetition of personal and possessive pronouns indicates the structure of speaker and listener, almost like a dramatic monologue. The auxiliary verb 'would' introduces the hypothetical situation constructed in the first stanza: it has a conditional function, as does the entire first stanza. This helps the speaker to construct the textbook 'if – but – so' argument described above. The verb 'grow' refers to love on one level but also facilitates a descent into sexual innuendo and a certain crude wit. The growth here is most definitely of the erectile variety. An abrupt change of tone is signalled by the verb 'hear' in the opening line of the second stanza, which also signals a sensory change from the predominant visual imagery of the first stanza to the growing importance of aural imagery in the second. It all leads the reader to the tactile overload of the final stanza. The 'think' of the final line in the second stanza also signals the very personal and very subjective nature of the speaker's argument.

Even the length of the stanzas seems to reflect Marvell's mode of argument. The first stanza has 20 lines, which conjures a world where time is in abundance; the second stanza is the shortest, with only 12 lines, reinforcing the counter-argument of time as a non-renewable resource racing towards empty; and finally the last stanza contains 14 lines, which is somewhere between the utopia and dystopia of the previous two stanzas and promotes the idea of enjoying sensual pleasures. The three stanzas also relate to the form of the ode, which is a form that Marvell used for his *An Horatian Ode Upon Cromwell's Return from Ireland*. The function of the ode [long poems involving serious meditations in an elevated style] is highly unsuited to the content and style of this poem. However, the tri-partite structure of the Greek original seems to align with the tri-partite structure of this poem. The strophe, anti-strophe and epode of the Pindaric ode correspond with the hypothesis, anti-hypothesis and conclusion of Marvell's poem. Marvell's ironic use [or abuse] of a serious form connects to his inappropriate harassment of his mistress where he has everything to gain and she has everything to lose.

Opposites attract?

In a poem that relies on building contrast through oppositional states it is no surprise that the imagery follows suit. Given the tonal differences of each stanza it makes sense, for a change, to follow the chronology of the poem.

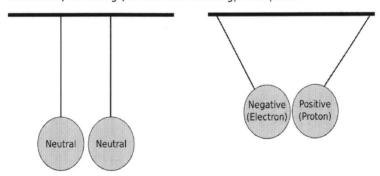

The first stanza is awash with imagery of the infinite, the gigantic. Everything found in the first stanza luxuriates in vastness and abundance. The tone established is one of playfulness and it is hard to take the speaker's words seriously. The hypothetical situation that he creates is one where Time itself is a luxury. This allows the speaker to appreciate his Lady's coyness, but it is also a subtle rejection of such coyness in reality. Marvell builds a contrast between the mistress strolling 'by the Indian Ganges' side' picking rubies. The opposition between seducer and seduced is underscored by the exotic imagery of India, which is juxtaposed abruptly with the more mundane images of the Humber, the estuary of Marvell's hometown of Hull, where the poet languishes. He presents us with a vast spatial contrast as well as a contrast in activities and colour. The Humber is known for its dark waters, which gives an effective contrast with the rubies his lover picks. While he complains, she picks precious stones. It appears to be sly praise, suggesting that his lover deserves such exotic climes due to her own high value. It also neatly equates the female with a beautiful, decorative commodity: the ruby. The choice of the ruby is also symbolic, where its colour carries connotations of passion and deep sensual energies.

This vastness of space is matched by a vastness of time. When the amorous speaker announces it will take from 'ten years before the Flood … Till the conversion of the Jews' for their seduction to take place he spans from early Biblical times until some far off point in the future. This luxury of time is broken down when the speaker deconstructs his lover's body and dedicates great swathes of time to adoring each. The quick switch from non-sexualized to sexualized parts [i.e. from 'eyes' to 'breast'] signals seductive rather than courtly motivation. This is also reinforced by the clever sexual innuendo of 'my vegetable love should grow / Vaster than empires'. As we've suggested, the vegetable in question is rather phallic in shape and continues to 'grow' as the male gaze becomes fixated on the sexual parts of the woman's body. Equating 'love' and 'rate' can be interpreted as purely quantitative i.e. the Lady deserves such gigantic flattery, it is a form of payment to her beauty. More worryingly, love or sex is thus equated with financial terminology, which reflects the financial nature of marriage in this period but also strays into the territory of love as a sort of prostitution. This slyly cynical view observes that sex between man and woman is merely a transaction that is not strictly physical i.e. pleasure for pleasure, rather for the man to obtain sex he must pay with something the woman desires. Possibly the rubies mentioned in the beginning stages? Or just jewelled words.

Lying on your back [Take #1]

With this hypothetical flattery ringing in his Lady's ears the speaker then takes a sudden jarring change in tonal direction. The second stanza's opening 'But' obliterates the leisurely, sensuous ambling of the previous stanza. Marvell

introduces the opposite sensation: Time is hunting them down in its 'winged chariot'. Feelings of persecution are exacerbated by the new barren landscape: the 'Deserts of vast eternity' contrast very strongly with the exotic 'Indian Ganges' and lush 'vegetable love' of the previous stanza. Upping the persuasive intensity, Marvell moves swiftly from utopia to dystopia,

from making love to his Lady to the 'marble vault' of her tomb. It's not subtle but it is effective. Marvell moves from abundance of time to scarcity of time in a poetic charge that trails gothic imagery galore in its wake.

The speaker changes tactic: deny me too long and death will have you ... and your beauty. Specific details employed by the speaker are shocking: in this scenario, it is the worms not the speaker who will test her defences. The phallic symbolism of the worms as well as the messy equation of death and sex would set any decent Freudian student's heart racing! The patronizing 'quaint honour' described by the speaker is shown to be a needless pretence: virgin or not your flesh will be penetrated upon death. To choose a man over a swarm of worms seems to be the obvious and less disgusting choice. Of course, the hypocrisy of a male criticising the very concept imposed upon women by such men as himself points to the sexual double standards of the 17th century. The equation of 'honour' with 'dust' and 'ashes' with 'lust' echoes the funeral service: 'ashes to ashes, dust to dust...' This reinforces the deathly pallor of the stanza in general, and the process of decay in particular, but also universalizes the theme of transience and bodily desire. In this case, death can be equated with aging, i.e. the death of physical beauty. Again, this echoes a very familiar argument: enjoy physicality while you have it, it won't be here forever.

Marvell writes in rhyming couplets, which gives the poem a strong forward momentum. While not technically heroic couplets [rhyming couplets written in iambic pentameter], it could be argued that he writes in unheroic couplets by shaving two syllables off his poetic line. This suits the distinctly unheroic content of the poem, but also gives the poem a swiftness that the heroic couplet cannot instil. He employs a very regular iambic tetrameter throughout the entire poem, a metre also used to great effect in Marvell's *The Garden*.

> We would / sit down / and think / which way
> To walk / and pass / our long / love's day.

This regular metre reflects the unrelenting nature of the speaker's argument in trying to seduce his mistress but also reflects the universality of this seductive process. There are two notable exceptions to the strict iambic tetrameter metre. In the second stanza, there are 9 syllables in 'Thou by the Indian Ganges' side', which is a way of making it stand out from the mundane familiarity of the 'Humber'. Significantly, the other notable deviation comes early in the decasyllabic 'Time's winged chariot hurrying near'. Here the extra syllables are negated by the narrow vowels in 'chariot' and 'hurrying' so that the line seems to hurry over the extra beat. Here the poem begins its reflection on serious matters: time, mortality, life, death, existence itself. Lovemaking is no longer the only theme. But it is not forgotten either.

Lying on your back [Take #2]
With the inescapable logic established by contrasting two extreme states the speaker merely has to spell out the obvious for his Lady: IF only we had time...BUT we don't...SO, let's make the most of it while we can! Now the lovers are assumed to join forces not only for their mutual pleasure but also for their common, and universal, goal of defying Time itself. This final stanza is packed with action verbs: 'sport', 'devour', 'tear', 'run'. The thrill of the chase associated with sexual union has now been enlarged to encompass a larger chase, the thrill of defying Time by

packing as much experience into life as possible. The beginning of the stanza establishes a delicate sense of transience, where the 'youthful hue' of his Lady's beauty is about to evaporate. The imagery of 'amorous birds of prey' is another potentially disturbing equation that reinforces relations between men and women as that of predator and prey. The sensual overload of 'devour', 'tear' and 'roll' signals the sensual change from cold tomb to hot bed, from 'echoing song' to tactile heaven. While the image of the 'ball' introduces a sense of strength through togetherness, almost like a hedgehog rolling into a ball to ward off predators. In this case, Time is the predator not the male and the prey is the couple rather than the female. The 'sun' and its gendering as male alludes to classical myth, where Apollo is the sun god who traverses the heavens in a flaming chariot. This personification of the sun, and hence Time itself, turns the contest from gender based to a more universal theme altogether: Mortality itself. The triumphant final couplet preaches carpe diem: seize the moment and take control. Rather than be a passive victim of Time, become Time's master!

Weaknesses of sound, will and flesh

Marvell's rhyming couplets create a sense of certainty in the rhyme scheme though the use of strong, masculine rhyme i.e. 'time' and crime', obviously reflecting the confidence of the speaker in his argument's persuasive powers. When Marvell uses weaker, slant rhymes they are quite jarring; little sonic snags on the ear. What is more interesting are the words that are emphasized by these slant rhymes: 'lie', 'eternity', 'try' and 'virginity'. In fact these couplets look to be split deliberately; surely 'lie' would be much more suitably paired with 'try' and 'eternity' with 'virginity'. Marvell seems to be playing with these words in a clever but obscure way. Perhaps getting the reader to focus on these four words makes him/her play around with the combinations and come to conclusions that Marvell wants us to consider; maybe that virginity is overrated and is, as such, a lie, or maybe that we should try striving for eternity by cramming our days with as much experience as we can. Maybe the complexity of the words 'virginity' and 'eternity' are the words he wants the reader to ruminate upon as they are complex concepts themselves leading to all types of discussions on love and gender, behavioural norms and time, mortality and decay etc. Ultimately, the weakness in sound patterns also connects to the wider thematic concerns of natural human weakness regarding indulgence of natural desires and also the weakness of the flesh in defying mortality.

The sounds of seduction

In terms of sound patterns Marvell employs assonance in the form of long vowel sounds, especially in the first stanza. This makes sense as the long "O"s of "world

enough", "long love", "before the flood" and "more slow" has the effect of slowing the pace. This makes poetic sense as the central idea of the first stanza is to create a scenario where time is not an issue, where the pace is languid. Contrasting with this are the short vowels of the second stanza, particularly the buzzwords of 'eternity' and 'virginity', which quicken the pace and emphasise time is running out. Indeed, the final stanza is a sensual statement that delights in the pleasures of the flesh. Marvell uses sibilance, to create a hissing, sizzling noise that might be appropriate to the hotbed of physical activity that dominates this final stanza:

- 'soul transpires / At every pore with instant fires'
- 'let us sport us [...] amorous birds of prey'
- 'sweetness"; our sun / Stand still.'

It may also be a way of creating a sense of deflation, of loss suggesting transience and decay, which ultimately must spur the mistress and the reader to take life by the horns and wrestle for supremacy. Alternatively, this sound could be interpreted more positively; as a background whistling sound that mimics the excitement and swiftness of the chase.

Marvell also uses alliteration in places to add sonic flourishes to his poem. Notably he frontloads and endloads this poem with alliteration, which draws our ear to his hypothetical starting point and the emphatic declaration of the poem's denouement. So in the first four lines he provides alliteration as follows: 'we' and 'world'; 'coy' and 'crime'; 'we', 'would', 'way' and 'walk'; 'long' and 'love'. Proliferation of alliteration adds to the exotic beauty being described in the opening stanza. However, as Marvell progresses into the darker second stanza, all beauty is stripped away to reveal the gothic gloom of the tomb. However, he returns emphatically to alliteration in the final couplet, which adds further emphasis to his message. See the 'th's of 'Thus' and 'though' [which also connect back to the previous line's 'Thorough'], the 'st's of 'Stand' & 'still' and the 'w's of 'we' & 'will'. There is also notable consonance, with "n" and "m" sounds dominating, which lends the couplet's sound patterns a lovely soft smoothness.

To My Coy Crunching

TIME – COYNESS – SIT – LONG – INDIAN – RUBIES – COMPLAIN – FLOOD – REFUSE – CONVERSION – GROW – EMPIRES – PRAISE – EYES – ADORE – THOUSAND – AGE – HEART – DESERVE – RATE – ALWAYS – TIME'S – LIE – ETERNITY – BEAUTY – VAULT – WORMS – VIRGINITY – HONOUR – LUST – GRAVE – EMBRACE – YOUTHFUL – SKIN – WILLING – FIRES – SPORT – AMOROUS – DEVOUR – LANGUISH – ROLL – SWEETNESS – PLEASURES – LIFE – SUN – RUN

Other seduction poems in the anthology include *The Flea* and *The Scrutiny*. *La Belle Dame Sans Merci* and *Whoso List to Hunt* also feature actual or potential seductions and a predator-prey theme. Specious rhetoric, where the speaker tries to persuade someone through highly dubious logic, also features in *Absent from Thee*. Time as an adversary also crops up in *At an Inn*.

Richard Lovelace, *The Scrutiny*

Richard Lovelace has a surname ideal for his poem. Lovelace – pronounced Loveless – pronounces a rejection of one type of love for another and resents the stranglehold of romantic love itself. Like his rather interesting title of 'Gentleman Wayter Extraordinary' Richard seems obliged to perform a type of sexual servitude in this poem that is neither extraordinary or exciting. And truth be told, he's not very happy about it! Unsurprisingly, for a man 'much admired and adored by the female sex', Lovelace has quite a common blokey solution to his problem: leave and come back later. **The Scrutiny**, unfortunately, does not take an enlightened approach to gender relations -hardly a surprise given its genesis in 1642.

Love's for girls

This short poem has a pretty direct message for its reader: men need variety before settling down. It neglects to consider what women need at all, apart from a sly insinuation that women's insistence on monogamy gets in the way of natural desires.

The poem begins with a stinging rhetorical question that paints his 'lady' as a clinging constraint; her insistence that he 'swear' he is hers alone has drawn a petulant response. The speaker's statement that 'it is already morn' suggests that time is going quite slow for our impatient and inconstant lover. His description of pledging monogamous loyalty is described as a 'fond impossibility' where the adjective 'fond' seems to carry more negativity than usual. Here it suggests a sentimental simplicity at odds with the male's desire for a more fulfilling love life. Connecting this to the title, it's a 'scrutiny' of his intentions that our speaker clearly detests.

Whether the male Lothario in question has spent the night having sex with his Lady or *trying* to have sex with her is not exactly clear. This lack of sexual excitement however could not be clearer in his description of their time together as 'a tedious twelve  hours' space' – ouch! – no flattering 'how was it for you, my love?' here! Lovelace, cleverly suggests the tedium by adding an additional syllable into this line [as every other second line in the stanzas are hexasyllabic]. Additionally, when he enquires 'Have I not loved thee much and long?' the speaker implies his Lady is an ungrateful lover who neither appreciates his amorous antics or the size of his pleasuring device, as suggested by the euphemistic adverb 'long'. Not a modest or gallant man, our speaker!

It's not me, it's you

But why is our cavalier lover getting his pantaloons in such a twist? Not because his pleasures are being curtailed but because his Lady's pleasure are being curtailed. Of course. If she doesn't allow him to wander then she will foolishly 'rob [herself] of a new embrace'. It's not the most elegant attempt at reverse psychology seen in the history of English letters, but at least it's blatant. It does, however, suffer from a crucial flaw in its argument: by assuming that man and woman desire a polyamorous existence it conflates the attitudes of both lovers.

Regardless of this highly flawed logic our bored lover ploughs on with this argument and goes onto illustrate how much there is to gain from this life philosophy. Naturally, he spends the next half of the poem discussing how much he will gain without bothering to consider his Lady again.

Sexist synecdoche

For a young man adored by the female sex and rampaging round the 1640s, it is entirely predictable that his views on women are of the patriarchal variety. At the start of the third stanza, the speaker reduces all women to a dehumanising categorisation based on colour. In an oddly sexless synecdoche where women are reduced to hair colour, the speaker declares that he is certain that not 'all joy' can be located 'in thy brown hair'. So obviously, logically and conveniently he must 'search the black and fair' to seek out joy too. The underwhelming range of female diversity encompassed by 'brown [...] black and fair' also shows a rather limited view of women as no more than objects or as a sum of their parts.

In a further objectification, Lovelace paints himself as a collector of women or more accurately the pleasures they give him. A familiar binary of active male desiring subject and passive female desired object is presented when the imagined future lovers are described as 'treasure'. It is a poem curious in its lack of imaginative imagery – it is mostly quite literal in its declarations.

The metaphor of the male lover as 'skilful mineralist' stands out, not because of its ingenious metaphysical brilliance, but because of a scarcity of vibrant imaginative imagery. The roving lover as a seventeenth century equivalent of a metal-detector wielding opportunist is an odd one but it is appropriately phallic. The image of the female as passive earth, hiding her inner treasures from the invasive and penetrating ploughman lover is quite a disturbing one in its suggestions of violation and exploitation. Such gendering of female nature and male domination is common in Western literature, most memorably in the Romantic poets' gendering of female nature/physicality and male imagination/intellect. Not only does Lovelace's image of the pillaging 'mineralist' connote males sowing their oats, it also suggests the libidinous male lover as an aggressive thief mining precious female valuables. In a time when women's social reputation was based on their suitability for wifehood, such rakish behaviour not only robs them of virginity but also of social status. Typical of the sexual double standards of patriarchal societies only the male gains from sexual experience while the woman loses in a very real sense: the labels of player and slut are centuries old and even today continue to deny the validity and equality of female sexual desires.

Conquistador of the heart

This idea of gender relations as defined by conflict and a type of violence is

continued in the final stanza when Lovelace delivers a triumphant potential return to his Lady. Like a Roman general returning with the spoils of war, the male lover is imagined a 'laden' 'with the spoils of meaner beauties'. The adjective 'laden' certainly highlights to his Lady that he's not one for moderation. The noun 'spoils', while certainly meaning the rewards he has rakishly collected [again continuing the metaphor of 'skilled mineralist'] also has a darker, more disturbing meaning when used as a verb. Rather than concentrating on the material valuables the verb reveals the way in which they are obtained. The verb 'to spoil' in previous usage is more akin to our modern understanding of verbs like 'pillage' or 'plunder'. Hence the spoils the male lover hungrily hypothesises imply wrongful actions associated with stripping a place of valuables [there is also an obvious connection with the literal stripping of the female body also]. The war-time usage of such language again emphasises the conflict laden aspects of sexual relations between men and women.

However, our speaker, like every good patriarch, doesn't concern himself too much with the distresses of a female. He may [if he's that bothered] return to his lady 'crowned', thus portraying himself as some type of rakish royal – a love king of epic experience. The fact that this return is strictly provisional confirms the gigantic ego that makes these claims. Our lucky Lady can only look forward to embracing such a lady-killer if she 'prov'st the pleasant she'. What an odd adjective to describe the winner of his heart – it makes one reflect on what he's looking for in all his other conquests: tolerable, presentable, downright unpleasant?! He's not that fussy, as long as he has 'variety' and a suitably long innings ['when I have loved my round']. The wording of the final line is intriguing where 'Ev'n' suggests a rampant male sexual appetite that is almost insatiable, as opposed to the 'sated' the speaker claims. It probably doesn't bode well for the marriage of our young lovers – assuming his lordship returns in the first place! Lovelace cleverly suggests this sexual overload in this final line with its additional syllable and extra beat and thereby adding 'variety' to his standard iambic tetrameter lines.

Forms of variety in variety of form?

For a poem with a distinct lack of killer imagery, devoid of memorable sound patterning or presenting a complex theme, the form that Lovelace employs is unusual. His meditations on sexual freedom are constrained by four cinquains or quintets [5-line stanzas]. These cinquains are cross-rhymed, which gives them a clear forward momentum until we hit the final line, which brings a contradictory sense of stasis as the rhyme scheme is ABABB [Long, Space, Wrong, Embrace, Face]. Thus, there's tension between moving on and staying still, almost a dramatisation of the conflicting male and female wills in the poem; the male wants to move on, the female wants the male to stay put. The rigidity of the form together with the short octasyllabic lines frame the speaker's boundless desires in a tight, constraining form that reflects the speaker's frustration at being 'forsworn'.

Inclusion of a hexasyllabic second line in each stanza is also a curious variation, signalling a loss of poetic energy with the loss of a beat only for that energy to re-establish itself in the next line. It almost shows a weakening of the speaker's resolve to indulge his desires and instead remain loyal to his lady. However, their rarity in the poem proves these are but momentary lapses and, together with the unrelenting message of the poem, we are left in no doubt as to what the speaker will prioritise: selfish indulgence. This deviation from the standard octocyllabic, iambic tetrameter lines that dominate the poem provides a variety of sorts. But again it seems an inadequate formal gesture to the type of wild sexual energies of the speaker. Clearly then, the form and message of the poem are in tension or conflict with one another; maybe a reflection of the battle between what the speaker wants and what society or loverly etiquette expects of him.

The Crunch

FORSWORN – VOWED – MORN – NIGHT – IMPOSSIBILITY – LONG – TEDIOUS – WRONG – ROB – DOTE – JOY – OTHERS – SEARCH – MINERALISTS – TREASURE – IF – PLEASANT – SPOILS – LADEN – VARIETY

The idea of returning to the beloved once other appetites have been sated links this poem to *Absent from Thee*. The tendentious and rhetorical nature of the poem connects it poems such as *To his Coy Mistress* and *The Flea*. This is also a poem about parting, as is *Ae Fond Kiss*.

John Wilmot, 2nd Earl of Rochester, *Absent from thee*

A rake's progress

Scan a potted biography of John Wilmot, the Earl of Rochester, and a few especially striking details leap from the page: It was as a student at Oxford University, for instance, that Wilmot apparently first 'grew debauched'. Nothing that shocking there you might think, if you didn't know that Wilmot was only 13 years old at the time. A little later, a little older, but apparently no wiser, he 'spectacularly abducted' the rich heiress Elizabeth Male and ended up locked in The Tower of London for his pains. Another time, in a drunken fit of rage Wilmot attacked King Charles II's prized sundial from the royal collection of astronomical instruments, hacking at with his sword until it was utterly destroyed. Charles was not pleased; Wilmot was banished. Following another unfortunate drunken incident in which one of his friends was killed with a pike thrust, the Earl briefly fled, disguised as one "Doctor

Bendo". 'Under this persona, he claimed skill in treating "barrenness" [infertility], and other gynaecological disorders.' Apparently this 'practice was "not without success", implying his intercession of himself as surreptitious sperm donor'. On other occasions, Rochester also 'assumed the role of the grave and matronly Mrs. Bendo, presumably so that he could inspect young women privately without arousing their husbands' suspicions'. In the end 'years of drinking - and sexual abandon with everyone one from great ladies to street whores - took their toll'. Indeed. By the age of 33 Wilmot was dead, killed by a toxic mixture of sexual diseases and alcoholism.

An archetypal rake, Rochester, clearly was a 'party animal' of the Restoration court, the opulence and lavishness of which was a reaction against the restrictive moral rules set out by the Puritan era. Britain had gone through an 'interregnum' [a period of time without a monarchy] as Charles I had been executed some years before at the climax of the English Civil War. The new court was a celebration of instant gratification and aristocratic flamboyance.

Described in his time as 'the wickedest man alive' Wilmot's lewd, dissolute rakish life hangs over his work. But there is another side to the libidinous Earl rather obscured by his notorious mad-cap antics and riotous revelry. Throughout his brief life Wilmot ping-ponged from being adored to reviled, frequently banished he was as frequently re-instated as a courtier by King Charles II. Nonetheless the poet satirised the King in heroically scathing, unflinching verse, such as in these memorable lines: 'Restless he rolls about from whore to whore/ a merry monarch, scandalous and poor'. Such frankness is bracing and, of course, highly dangerous. It should tell you a lot about Rochester's poetry that it was widely censored in the Victorian era.

There is lots of poetry written in this era that presents physical desire as superficial [for a great example look at *The Rape of The Lock* by Alexander Pope published a while later in 1712]. Reading this poem do you think the speaker is indecisive? What do you think the speaker is more controlled by - head or heart? Many of Wilmot's poems are satirical and concern the impossibility of sating his enormous appetite for life. In this poem, tongue firmly in cheek, he begs his beloved to be allowed to leave her so that he can engage in whatever 'torments' his 'fantastic mind' can conceive and then to be allowed eventually come back to her. In short, he tries to persuade her that he should be allowed to have his carnal cake and also eat it.

An unfixed heart

A common image in poetry, especially from the Renaissance and the Restoration, is that of the Petrarchan woman. This is what we call a woman who is described as being distant, or unattainable - it comes from Renaissance adaptations of the sonnets of Petrarch, a Roman poet. Rochester uses the idea of an unattainable woman a lot in his work, and we'll look at how this increases the yearning and longing that's communicated by the text. [The picture above is of Petrarch, looking suspiciously like a Petrarchan woman].

The Restoration court, for its celebration of instant pleasure and the use of words and humour for entertainment, was a creator of its own problems - if the things that make you happy don't last for very long each time you have them, it's easy to feel like you don't have a firm, permanent sense of 'home' or belonging somewhere stable. All the way through this poem, the speaker is the 'straying fool' that zig-zags between lots of different places - first he's absent from the person he loves, then in their arms, then flying from their arms, then going back to their 'safe bosom', where they 'expire'.

Both the speaker and the structure of the poem itself seem to be looking for somewhere stable, for some reconciliation. The metre of the poem reflects this. There are four beats in each line but the beats are not in a perfect or consistent rhythm- each stanza comes to a full stop and re-gathers itself before launching off again in the next one. Towards the end of the poem there are more strong beats, suggesting a finality - 'faithless to thee, false, unforgiven'. The rhymes also become more harmonious as the poem goes on; whereas they start as half-rhymes and don't quite match up [for example return/mourn], they match more closely at the end [unblest / rest]. The words of the poem and how they develop mirror the peace that the speaker hopes to find in the 'safe bosom' he's looking for.

Rochester populates his poem with the language of violence and sickness, like 'languish', 'mourn', 'torments', 'tears', 'wearied', 'woe', and 'expire'. Love is

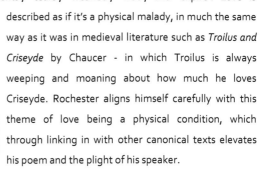

described as if it's a physical malady, in much the same way as it was in medieval literature such as *Troilus and Criseyde* by Chaucer - in which Troilus is always weeping and moaning about how much he loves Criseyde. Rochester aligns himself carefully with this theme of love being a physical condition, which through linking in with other canonical texts elevates his poem and the plight of his speaker.

Rochester wrote lots of poetry on the subject of women that he didn't feel secure about, and the failure of women or drink on indeed life to sate his appetite. <u>What effect does using the image of the unattainable woman have? How might this reflect the political situation at the time that Rochester was writing?</u>

Love and religion

Literature is always composed with the influences of previous and contemporary literary traditions and practices. The speaker in Rochester's poem uses language influenced by religion and scripture in talking about where he might rest, for example 'love, peace and truth'. The sentence 'wandering from that heaven', and in fact the whole stanza, could be read as a prescient warning to the Satan of Milton's *Paradise Lost* [1667]. The intertwining of religious and erotic or romantic language is nothing new - in the Bible we find the same sadness and separation as we do in Rochester's poem: 'All night long on my bed I looked for the one my heart loves; I looked for him but did not find him... I will search for the one my heart loves' [*Song of Songs* 3:1-2]. Specifically, the listener or reader in the 17th century would have known perfectly well that Rochester is deliberately mixing up images of God with images of a sex worker, and that the 'torments' he wants to try are both satirising the puritanical practice of self-flagellation and also the more adventurous services offered in a town brothel.

The religious reading of the poem would be that the speaker knows that he does bad things, and that these have the capacity to damage his soul, and eventually 'lose his everlasting rest'. However, the speaker always knows that he can come back to the 'safe bosom [where] I retire / where love and peace and truth does flow', the woman's 'safe bosom' analogous for the unconditional love of God. It's difficult to know what Rochester's own religious beliefs were [and in any case you are not marked on biographical information] but he would have lived in a world saturated with religious narratives and with the church as a pervasive cultural infrastructure. The linking of religious and spiritual language to how Rochester writes about the desired woman suggests that her presence is always guaranteed and that she is the source of goodness and moral health for the speaker, for she stops him from 'wandering from that heaven [to...] some base heart unblest'. Audiences at the time would have been shocked by the casual conflation of church and sexuality.

The speaker is looking for peace and repose but is worried about choosing the wrong place to do that, about choosing 'some base heart unblest'. Whereas Dryden says that he 'attempt[s] from love's sickness to fly in vain' [Dryden, 1664], Rochester is saying that love's sickness restores the painful parting. The sense of belonging, repose and safety - whether emotional or sexual - is presented as a healing balm for the pain and uncertainty of 'straying' and of spending 'all day, all night' in mourning. The technique is almost bathos - using a lofty or grand poetic technique and immediately switching to something common or vulgar. In this case the 'common' and 'vulgar' is always loosely concealed beneath the veneer of sophisticated language.

The Age of Reason

The Age of Reason was the time in the 17th century when people were thinking about how we learn information. Some thought that we achieved knowledge through logic and reason alone, and some thought that we learned by our senses and by experience. There is the same tension in this poem between things we learn through experience [like the fact that the woman's bosom is 'safety' and full of 'love and peace'] and things we learn because we've thought logically about them [like the fact that if the poem's speaker strays too far he could become faithless and lose his 'everlasting rest']. The mind wants to experience 'torments it deserves to try' but knows logically that that would '[tear] my fixed heart from my love'. The overall effect is the same as the rhymes that don't quite sound the same; there are lots of different ways in which the speaker travels from one extreme to the other in this poem, all creating a conflicting and confused atmosphere.

The poem suggests that, actually, physical gratification and returning to a woman's affections achieve a higher and more worthy 'contentment'. Rochester uses the language of spiritual, unconditional and almost 'holy' love to justify the transcendence that can be achieved through physical pleasure. <u>Does the poem succeed, do you think, in arguing this?</u>

A satirical old goat?

Strip the poem's argument down and re-phrase it in less poetic language and it's really not very convincing is it. Clearly the beloved has requested the licentious poet return from whatever wandering/ philandering he's been up to. To which, striking a suitably contrite and tragic tone, one arm raised dramatically against his brow, our protagonist replies:

Stanza 1: I'm really suffering, being separate from you, honestly. Please don't ask me when I'm coming home, 'cos that only makes me feel worse [sob]. →Stanza 2: If you let me continue to play away from home I'll be able to get all my mad [sexual] fantasies right out of my system, truly. →Stanza 3: And after that, well, I'll feel able to settle down with you, my one true darling. At which point he could/ should have stopped. But no, there's more:→Stanza 4: And otherwise [if I'm not allowed to do exactly what I like] I'll only end up wandering off again. And it'll be all your fault. You, my cruel love, will have made me 'false' and made me fall from 'heaven', killing my soul. And you don't want that, now do you? So...

 How about writing the lady's reply? What language might she use? Would she be as courtly and religious as Wilmot's or would she, perhaps, be a bit more frank and direct?

Absent from thee crunched:

ABSENT – LANGUISH – FOOL – WISH – MOURN – FLY – MIND – TORMENTS – HEART – LOVE – WEARIED – WOE – RETIRE – LOVE – EXPIRE – HEAVEN – UNBLEST – FAITHLESS – REST

Other poems that can be connected with this with the themes of wanting something [or someone] unattainable or unavailable are: *She Walks in Beauty*, *The Flea*, *Whoso List to Hunt* and *Remember*.

William Blake, *The Garden of Love*

Dissenter

noun

plural noun: dissenters

- A person who dissents
- A member of a non-established church; a non-conformist; freethinker.

Poet, engraver and painter William Blake [1757-1827] was certainly a dissenter. An anti-authoritarian political radical and bold artistic original, Blake rejected the teachings of contemporary Christianity. Marginalised and considered by some to be mad in his own time, Blake has come to be seen as one of England's greatest visionary artists. He did not, however, merely dissent. Blake was a revolutionary, hellbent on transforming society and the human spirit, and, in order to do this, he had to combat what he called the 'abomination' of 'false religion'. In the words of Professor Robert Ryan:

'Blake's usual religious posture ... is not submission but protest; his poetry is a sustained prophetic denunciation of the cruelties, mental and corporeal everywhere perpetuated in the name of God by those who claim to be doing his will. It is a detailed indictment of the collaboration of all the churches in the exploitation of the poor, the degradation of labor, the subordination of women, the abridgement of political liberty, the repression of sexual energy, and the discouragement of original in the fine arts' [8]

Blake was, however, deeply Christian. In contrast to what he considered a deformed and corrupt state relligion, his Christianity was centred on the figure of Jesus and on championing social justice, creative freedom and mutual love. In particular, as we see in *The Garden of Love*, Blake rejected the Church's connection of sex with sin. For Blake, sexual intercourse was natural, joyful and essentially divine.

Unlike contemporary fellow Romantic poets, such as Wordsworth and Coleridge William Blake was not university educated - in fact he left school when he was just ten years old- and he did not come from the middle classes. Blake was a working class artisan who trained as an engraver. Nor was his poetry printed by friends or through literary connections. Blake wrote, illustrated, engraved and printed his books himself and sold remarkably few copies in his life time. Nowadays, of course, the few extant copies of *Songs of Innocence and Experience,* from which collection *The Garden of Love* is taken, are priceless. Disdaining contemporay taste, Blake  always claimed he was famous 'in eternity'. From a modern perspective it seems, perhaps, that he was right.

I won't do what you tell me

So, how does *The Garden of Love* reflect Blake's radicalism? In two major ways; through its style and through its challenging central idea or theme. For a contemporary audience, schooled on the works of Augustan poets who valued

---

[8] Robert Ryan, *Blake and religion* in The Cambridge Companion to Blake.

elegant construction and satirical wit above all else, Blake's style must have seemed extraordinary direct, bare and rough. Whereas Augustan poetry aimed to entertain and delight, Blake's poetry aims to touch the reader's heart and spark it into action. Whereas Augustan poetry developed a heightened poetic language, or diction, to help distinguish it from mere prose, Blake, like Wordsworth, strips poetry of inflated ormamentation, using instead ordinary, everyday, artisan words bolted together like sheets of metal.

Tak ethe first stanza. The verbs are some of the simplest and most common in English, 'went', 'saw', 'seen', 'was', 'used', 'play'. The vast majority of all the words are basic monosyllables; ony 'garden', 'never' and 'chapel' are not, and these are hardly complex. There are very few descrptive words, such as adjectives, and no metaphors or similes. Nor, in fact, are there any other obvious poetic devices. The construction of the two sentences is also simple, each with two parts fused by a monosyllabic conjunction, first 'and' and then 'where'. Superficially at least, this is language a child could understand. Indeed, Blake originally intended *Songs of Innocence* to be for children and he wanted these poems to be accessible to a wide audience.

If the first stanza is characterised then by directness and simplicity, it is also roughly constructed in regards to its metrics. Generally, conventially, it was considered good poetic style to stick to one dominant metre in a poem, like keeping to a time signature in music. The result of mixing metres would be a poem that stumbled and tripped itself up. Scanning Blake's poem reveals how irregular and unconventional it is. Stressed syllables are in bold:

'I **went** to the **Gard**en of **Love**'

The poem opens with a two beat foot, an iamb, unstress / stress. But immediately Blake deviates into three beat anapests, unstress / unstress / stress. The pattern is, however, fairly clear and pronounced. The same pattern is repeated in the rest of the stanza:

'And **saw** what I **ne**ver had **seen**
A **chap**el was **built** in the **midst**
Where I used to **play** on the **green'**

Technically we have here a slight variation of anapestic trimeter [with the first unstressed foot docked] a curious and unusual metre that creates immediate forward momentum. The metre helps, in fact, to convey the suddeness of the transformation the poet experiences.

In the second stanza an extra syllable is added to each line and the metre becomes knottier and harder to distinguish. Where, for instance, do the stresses fall in 'And thou shalt not writ over the door'? Some lines have extra beats, becoming tetrameters. The last line of the second stanza certainly has four beats:

'That so **man**y **sweetflow**ers **bore'**

As Stephen Fry has commented elsewhere on Blake's metrics, even by the end of the second short quatrain of *The Garden of Love* the metre is rather 'shot to pieces'. The most radical irregularity, however, comes in the poem's final two lines:

'And **priests** in **black** <u>gowns</u> were **walk**ing their <u>**rounds**</u>
And **bind**ing with <u>briars</u> my **joys** and <u>de**sires**</u>.'

It is clear, visibly, that the first of these lines sticks out unitidily from the rest of the poem. Far longer, with three excess syllables, it could be scanned as either a tetrameter or, longer still,as a pentameter, as we have done. The radical shifting ground of these lines is also, of course, signalled by the abrupt switch to internal rhyme from the previously established end rhyme. An unsettling effect is enhanced by the marked use of echoic effects, particularly alliteration of the 'b's and assonance of the 'i' vowel sound in the last line, running through 'bi', 'bri', 'my' and 'si', creating a binding of words through sound. The poem seems to bring us up short, tightening up and coming to an end before we expect it.Of course, this sonic tightening fits with and emphasises the final image of constriction.

To some purists [and pedants] Blake's metrical looseness and roughness might be considered to reveal a sign of lack of skill, or weakness or characteristic eccentricity. For us,however, Blake's generation of disturbance within the quatrain form is deliberate and highly effectve. The reader is not allowed to fall into a familiar or regular pattern of reading and the poem takes us on a rather bumpy ride to an unexpected place.

Bricks of religion

Blake does not seek to hide or obscure his radical message. His poem is starkly direct. An innocent, natural world of love has been destoyed by conventional religion. Freedom, beauty and play have been replaced by prohibition, surveillance and imprisonment. Notice how the emphatic, monosylabic phrase 'Thou shalt not' is not attached to any specific action or phrase. Rather

it expresses a general state of mind, emphasising blanket authoritarian control. The Chapel is also exclusive and excluding; its gates are 'shut', presumably to keep out the common folk of the green.

Indeed its arrival seems to have poisoned the green. The symbolic flower, connoting procreation and natural beauty, is replaced by 'tomb-stones' and 'graves'. Priests dressed in black guard the chapel, 'walking their rounds'. Blake employs a number of symbols that crop up elsewhere in his poetry. Priests, in particular, come in for a lot of stick. In the picture on the next page, from Blake's design for this poem, the priest seems be teaching the girl and boy piety, which probably does not seem too terrible.They are, however, boxed into a symbolically dark and cramped space, perhaps a crypt, somewhere underground at any rate. It is a sombre-looking image, with a gloomy pallete, of a place that is the polar opposite of a vibrant, open green where children can play and grow freely. In *The Marriage of Heaven and Hell* Blake is more explicit about what he deems priests' baleful influence, comparing them to insects destroying leaves: 'As the caterpillar chooses the fairest leaves to lay her eggs on, so the priest lays his curse on the fairest joys'. Worst of all, with 'trembling zeal' a priest, in *A Little Boy Lost*, executes a small boy, burning him alive in a 'holy place'.For Blake priests were agents of the state and sometimes brutal enforcers of false religion. False religion especially feared sex. As the image at the start of this essay suggests, Blake associated flowers with sex. Hence the chapel and its priests destroy the flowers. Images of 'rounds' also feature prominently in Blake's work and usually suggest a closed way of thinking or behaving.

The metaphor of 'binding with briars' his 'joys and desires' is particularly powerful and resonates with many other images of imprisonment, physical or mental in Blake's poetry. Perhaps most famous is his image of indoctrination, of brain-washing, in *London* where the populace are described as suffering 'mind-forg'd manacles'. The metaphor is similar in *The Garden of Love*, but, perhaps this binding is more disturbing. The fact that 'briars' are used suggests both that the priests manage to turn nature against Blake and that they are able to make restriction seem natural and therefore unchallengeable. The most effective indoctrination is, of course, invisible to the victim. Notice too that Blake uses the participle 'binding' rather than the past tense of 'bound'. Ominously, the particle indicates that the oppression will be continuous and unending.

Many of the poems of **Songs of Experience** have a matching or echoing poem in *Songs of Innocence*. For *The Garden of Love* the poetic twin is *The Echoing Green*. Reading the Innocence poem helps clarify the symbolism of 'the green'. As we have already suggested, the green is a place of childhood play, freedom and joy, a kind of village utopia or pastoral idyll.Blake was an artist, of course, and the colour green connoted fertility, life and natural energy for him. The green is a sort of Eden before the Fall. In the Experience poem the world of the green has been utterly changed. Perhaps this is because the Chapel has been built and the priests moved in – Blake's London was changing fast and becoming increasingly industrialised. But another way of seeing this transformation is as embodying a change in perspective and perception of the narrator. Their original, innocent reading of the world around them has given way to a more experienced and jaundiced perspective. Psychologically, in growing up, they have experienced a sort of Fall, an eviction from the garden. For Blake, as for all the Romantics, children were closest to God and the process of growing up and of socialisation was a form of corruption. False religion was the key source of this corruption.

The Garden of Love crunch

LOVE – NEVER – CHAPEL – PLAY – SHUT – NOT – GARDEN – FLOWERS – GRAVES – SHOULD – PRIESTS – BINDING

Many other poems present barriers to love, including *Whoso List to Hunt*, *Sonnet 116*, *The Flea* and *Ae Fond Kiss*. The control of sex, albeit by different agents, is also prominent theme in *The Scrutiny*. *The Ruined Maid* explores society's corruption of innocence. And an interesting comparison could also be made in terms of the style of Blake's poem with that of another Romantic poet, Keats's, *La Belle Dame sans Merci*.

Robert Burns, *Ae Fond Kiss*

Ev'ry time we say goodbye

People have gone mad for ***Ae Fond Kiss*** ever since Robert Burns wrote it in 1791, and had it published a year later in The Scots Musical Museum. Probably only the New Year's Eve club anthem, *Auld Lang Syne*, pulls in more royalties for the Burns estate, and that's just a matter of branding more than anything. The novelist Sir Walter Scott called AFK 'exquisitely affecting,' adding that it 'contains the essence of a thousand love tales,' and modern critics have tended to agree: G. Ross Roy dubbed it 'one of the greatest love songs in the language,' while David Daiches wrote that 'in it, with the skill so characteristic of love poetry at its best, Burns reduces everything to one basic and overpowering emotion, the emotion of having loved and now having to part.'

Ringing endorsements all; and elicited in part, no doubt, by the autobiographical content underpinning the words: a true story of love and loss from Burns' life, which inevitably lends added intrigue and gravity to the poem. The story went as follows: Burns had come to Edinburgh in 1787 to supervise the republication of his collection, Poems, Chiefly in the Scottish Dialect, and found that Poems had made him something of a celebrity among the aristocratic and literary circles of Edinburgh. Among their number was Mrs Agnes Maclehose, a married woman whose estranged and unloving husband had long been living in Jamaica, and she found herself immediately drawn to Burns, and he to her. They exchanged letters, increasingly intense, but, owing to Maclehose being a] a married woman, and b] of a higher class than Burns, social conventions made the relationship impossible. **Ae Fond Kiss** was written after the pair's final, sorrowful meeting, before Maclehose would travel to Jamaica to rejoin her husband.

A touching story of true love's course running rough. And, for many, one of the most touching love songs on the market. The 'heart-wrung tears' of the first stanza are classic lovelorn stuff, as are the 'sighs and groans' of the next line. The image of the infinite, lightless universe, devoid of the 'cheerfu' twinkle' of a 'star of hope', where 'Dark despair' descends all around, seems to get stuck in people's throat. And the substitution of 'alas!' for 'and then' in the otherwise exact repetition of the first four lines, which implies an involuntary eruption of deepest feeling in the otherwise controlled versification, brings a tear to the collective eye. Moving, too, is the present tense of 'Ae fond kiss, and then we sever' which, given that the words were written after the couple's last meeting, seems designed to keep that final kiss alive indefinitely, or at least to prolong it. And the title of Most Stirring Four Lines is often awarded to:

'Had we never lov'd sae kindly,
Had we never lov'd sae blindly,
Never met – or never parted –
We had ne'er been broken-hearted,'

Note the intricate job which the anaphora and rhyme-scheme do in making the lovers' causes of joy and agony inseparable: their 'kindly' [good, or natural] love can hardly be divorced from their rash 'blindness' to the inevitable consequences. The seed of their anguish, Burns acknowledges, was right there in the fruit of their bliss.

Don't you want me, baby?

But there's something else going on in those much-celebrated four lines, specifically in the line 'Never met – or never parted'. Burns uses long dashes, which he doesn't use anywhere else in the poem, to separate the clause, 'or never parted', as if he is trying to draw particular attention to it. And the significance of the words is unmistakable: though he has been railing against 'Fortune', as if the situation is  beyond mortal control, and has fused 'kindly' and 'blindly' in the manner described above, he can't help but lay the blame for the miserable circumstances on Agnes. It's her decision for them to part – she's the one sailing off to Jamaica – and all would be solved if she simply reversed her decision. It's a touch of finger-pointing and hostility which at first seems out of place in this most plaintive of love songs, until it becomes clear that there is pent-up aggression lurking behind pretty much every line. Beneath the poem's romantic overtures which generations of readers and critics have heard, there is a strain of anger and resentment.

Take the first line, the line by which the song is known: 'Ae fond kiss, and then we sever'. Clearly, 'and then we sever' means 'and then we part'; and yet 'sever' is a surprisingly violent choice of verb for the context, with its connotations of cutting, of physical mutilation. It could be that Burns wishes to evoke a particularly sudden and / or painful separation, of course, but it could also be that he wishes to establish from the outset an undertone of violence and combativeness. This aggro theory is strengthened when Burns qualifies the standard 'sighs and groans' with the unlikely adjective 'Warring', and seems to be confirmed when he ends that fourth line with the phrase, 'I'll wage thee', since 'wage' can mean 'promise', but is also regularly used in the context of 'waging war', initiating a conflict. Indeed, flanked by 'Warring' and 'wage', those commonplace 'sighs and groans' start to sound less like those of a broken-hearted lover than those of a soldier, nursing his injuries. It's almost as if Burns and Maclehose have taken up arms against each other, or at least the former against the latter.

Certainly, Burns is feeling aggrieved, and that interjection, 'or never parted', isn't the only instance of him subtly shifting the blame for the situation from Fate to Agnes. The second verse's first line, 'I'll ne'er blame my partial fancy', sees him doing the groundwork for the indictment, making it clear that it's not his fault, that he isn't the one to blame [even though he conceals it in the tones of helpless love: 'Naething could resist my Nancy']. Moreover, that phrase 'partial fancy' is really odd, and though people are often trying their best to twist it about and make it synonymous with 'true love', it isn't an easy fit. It's possible to argue that 'partial' means 'biased' or 'fond' [as in, 'I'm partial', but it's unlikely that Burns was unaware of the word's other meaning: minor, or incomplete. 'Fancy', too, though often used to signify an amorous inclination [and even then it's not a particularly strong term, like 'love' or 'adoration'], can also stand for an illusion or a delusion, a transitory fascination, or an assumption based on no solid evidence. A minor romantic interest? Or a misguided delusion? Either way, this doesn't exactly sound like Burns being sincere and tender and heartfelt, aching with the loss of his one true love.

What it sounds like is someone slightly dismissing the significance of a relationship in order to get back a former lover who's abandoned them. The 'fond' and 'fareweel' of the opening lines have a tendency to sound a little formal, a little polite, a little less than passionate, as if the speaker is trying to imply the relationship was never much more than platonic, anyway. And that 'fond', if read as more romantic, is tinged with the word's other, less earnest connotations: silliness, childishness, playfulness. We know that Maclehose was far from Burns' only lover; is he trying to remind her of that? to imply that, to him, the relationship was just a light-hearted way to pass the time? The lines 'Thine be ilka joy and treasure, / Peace, enjoyment, love, and pleasure!' have been criticised for being weak and impersonal, the cheap words of valentine sentimentality, but surely this effect is deliberate: surely the bathetic, uninspiring list of some of life's 'treasures' is meant to communicate that, to an extent, at least, Burns isn't being sincere when he says he wishes her well.

Mo money mo problems
Burns' bitterness is clearly provoked not just by Maclehose's having left him, but more specifically by her having chosen her husband instead. He makes the unhappy love-triangle pretty explicit in the first verse, setting the rhyming words back from the ends of lines 3-8 so that pairs of significant words emerge: 'thee / thee', 'him / him', and 'me / me'. And it seems that he looks for ways to make Agnes feel guilty

about her decision, to insinuate that her choice was made for dubious reasons, in an attempt to make her reconsider, or just by way of retaliation.

Burns was, for example, the poorer and lower class of the two men in Maclehose's life, the Ayrshire son of a tenant farmer rather than a wealthy émigré. Throughout the poem there are hints that he feels Agnes has ditched romance and chosen the more financially-rewarding and socially-advantageous option. That unlikely word 'wage' in the first verse has yet another significance besides 'promise' and 'initiate conflict': the payment given to a person for completing a job. And 'pledge', the word in the previous line that pairs with 'wage', has a monetary meaning too: the payment of a debt / money or valuables deposited as a security in case of failure. In the same verse we get 'Fortune', which can mean 'Fate' but could mean 'riches', and in this context the 'twinkle' of the 'star of hope' looks a lot like the glitter of gold. As such, one reading of 'Me, nae cheerfu' twinkle lights me' might be 'I never have

much cash,' which would marry it with an interpretation of 'I'll ne'er blame my partial fancy' as 'I won't apologise for not being rich and upper class,' with 'fancy' standing, as sometimes it does, for 'wealth' and 'taste' and 'elegance'.

The first four lines of the third verse, too, seem to contain pretty dense [if veiled] accusations of avarice and snobbery. Is it any surprise, for example, that Burns gives 'treasure' as a synonym for the joys of life that Maclehose might enjoy? Or that 'dearest' can signify 'most expensive' as well as 'most beloved'? Burns' suggestion in that 'dearest' double entendre seems to be that Agnes is out of his price range, while 'Thine be ilka joy and treasure' could be read not only as 'I wish you every treasure', but also as 'Every treasure is yours already', i.e. 'You're already rich [while I'm not]'. When he says, 'thou first' and 'thou best', it seems to be a bit of a back-handed compliment, implying that she considers herself more important and is putting herself first. And, considering that 'fair' can mean 'pale-skinned', a physical characteristic traditionally limited to those who were wealthy enough not to have to work outside in the fields, 'fairest' sounds like a jibe against Maclehose's upper-class upbringing, her membership of an elite to which Burns could never belong.

You're gonna make me lonesome when you go

That Edinburgh elite had become very Anglicised by Burns' day, more like London society than the Scots of the Highlands, and this seems to be both part of Burns' grievance and part of his way of getting back at the former lover he feels has wronged him. Burns is regarded as the National Poet of Scotland in part because independent Scottish literature kind of died with him. A certain homogenisation of Scottish and English cultures had begun in earnest in 1603 when James VI of Scotland became James I of England, unifying the crowns, and it continued in 1707 with the merging of the Parliaments. By the time Burns was writing, aristocratic society and the literary culture were, at least in the big cities like Edinburgh, pretty much one and the same. Though the aristocracy and literati, including Agnes, admired the Scots vernacular of the 'ploughman poet', the non-English vocabulary  Burns used was becoming less and less intelligible to them. The 'Scottishness' of Maclehose and people like her was receding, and, moreover, she was abandoning Scotland for the New World.

That Burns imbues this love song with a strong Scots flavour, therefore, is simultaneously seductive and hostile: it bears the Scots features which the upper-classes had fetishised, while at the same time making deliberately alien a poem which at first appeared to be entirely personal, written in a letter to Maclehose, and including her nickname, 'Nancy'. For example, though Burns uses just six different Scots words in the song, he calls on the most distinctly Scots word, 'ilka', at the most significant moment: the moment when he is wishing her 'joy and treasure'. The subtext here seems to be, 'Not much chance you'll be finding ilka joy in

Jamaica, idiot'. The song, moreover, is written to fit a specific tune, 'Rory Dall's Port', a traditional Scots song which was composed by a blind harpist and bard of the Highlands, and belonged much more to Burns' Ayrshire than Agnes' Edinburgh, and much less the Jamaica she was sailing for. And the unusual metre of the song, which is trochaic tetrameter, four metrical feet of stress / unstress per line, seems to be a knowing reversal of the iambic pattern which is often said to be the natural cadence of English. In the very foundations of the song, then, in the very arrangement of the most basics building-blocks of verse, Burns is turning his back on England, on Anglicised Edinburgh society, and on the upper-class woman whom he had loved and who now was leaving him behind.

Ae Fond Kiss crunched:

SEVER – FAREWEEL – PLEDGE – WAGE – FORTUNE – STAR – TWINKLE – DARK – PARTIAL – FANCY – RESIST – KINDLY – BLINDLY – PARTED – FAIREST – BEST – DEAREST – ILKA – TREASURE – PLEASURE

Lord Byron, *She Walks in Beauty*

Lord Byron- or George Gordon Byron- is another love poet in this collection with a notorious reputation. Famously labelled 'mad, bad and dangerous to know', Byron was renowned for his flamboyance, lambasted for his louche lifestyle and chased for his huge debts. Following rumours of incest with his half-sister, he fled England, exiling himself in Europe and he died of a fever in Greece aged 36. During his life he was one of the second generation of Romantic poets, which included Percy Bysshe Shelley and John Keats.

This poem is famous for its rich lyricism compressed into such a short work. Byron's most famous other poems, such as *Don Juan* are epically long, but here we find complex language and imagery distilled into a pithy snapshot of a strange, liminal, dreamlike figure. It's not really a love poem; it's more of an infatuation or obsession poem. The fascination with which this woman is described is remarkably similar to those descriptions of nature's beauty which so captivated Romantic poets. More particularly, the Romantic poets' idea of nature is that it can sometimes lure you in with chilling and otherworldly power, just like the woman does in **She walks in**

Beauty. She's made into a 'type' by the vision of the poem's enraptured speaker, a generic desirable goal made more of an achievement through presenting her as distant, unattainable, mysterious.

Superficiality

Whilst it's true to say that the poem has lots of superficial elements, it's also true that it makes the most of these. Superficiality shines through the language. The curiously generic description of the woman is made delicate and one-dimensional by the fact that the speaker refuses to talk of anything else. The perfect metre of the opening lines, in particular, signals a surface-level perfection that can be delicately wobbled or disrupted, like the glassy surface of a pond in the wind- 'she walks in beauty, like the night/ of cloudless climes and starry skies'.

'Pure', 'cloudless', 'tender', 'sweet', 'at peace', 'innocent', this is a woman that does nothing but smile and be a vessel for grace and physical attractiveness- her only facial expressions are rather blank [like 'thoughts serenely sweet express'] and the time when her face appears at all engaged is where she has 'smiles that win' to remember 'days in goodness spent'. Those in the 19th century just as much as those in the 21st century knew perfectly well that a paragon such as this did not exist- Byron is painting with the literary brushes of sensuousness and physical experience to create the feelings of awe and perhaps real reverence for an idealised object, not a real woman.

Byron deliberately doesn't create a complex and multifaceted character, nor does he provide a snapshot of a heroine from one of his epic poems. This is a different exercise- he capitalises on the short structure he is using to paint a static image, suspended in time. An admirer of the Augustan poets Pope and Dryden, characteristically in this poetry Byron was a satirist. He could be withering, for instance, about his fellow Romantic Poets; habitually he referred to the Lake poets, Wordsworth and Coleridge, as the 'pond poets' and rather rudely renamed the former Turdsworth. Is there any part of this poem that comes across as satirical

Keep your distance?

Byron was a widely travelled man, especially with regard to the Far East; it is easy to see the sensory impact of rich and foreign lands on his work. Nowadays the description 'oriental' isn't really used, because the root of the word suggests that the east revolves round the West [and we know perfectly well that the West isn't the centre of the universe!] However, Byron uses language that would have typically conjured up images of the exotic, of the foreign, of the 'other', in a world where trading passages made exposure to the Far East increasingly easy, and where the East was seen as a world of danger, intrigue and dark magic.

The woman described in the poem is described as the 'night'. This is curious as the night is something that co-exists with day, but never coincides with it, shrouded by mystery and revolving as the dark face of the Earth- always chasing the sun. Byron talks about her delicate, ideal balance by describing 'one shade the more, one ray the less'- like the encroaching of night upon day. Like a pair of compasses, the woman occupies the place of night; removed, and slightly out of reach, yet always faithfully revolving around the light. Perhaps the speaker of the poem takes the place of the figure always separated from this mysterious woman, but always part of her presence; this would give the impression that the woman is removed and unattainable, and we know how much male love poets like talking about women who are aloof and unattainable!

Another interesting aspect of the woman's appearance is the emphasis on her darkness and her mystique. She is at once 'all that's best of dark and bright', at once being two things- seductive because of her glittering 'smiles that win, the tints that glow' but cloaked in 'shade' that makes her all the more alluring. Her 'raven tress' and the 'starry skies' indicate that impact of Orientalism on Byron's work- the attraction to something that is exotic and strange, and the fetishisation of other cultures because they seem so far away from our own. Women from other countries, especially Asia, were frequently fetishized in this way to create the narrative of their unattainability and therefore heighten the difficulty [and hence reward] of the 'conquest'.

For an example of how the Romantic poets in particular used Orientalism to aestheticise those from eastern countries, have a look at *Kubla Khan* by Coleridge. The paradise there, 'where blossomed many an incense-bearing tree', creates that same kind of still, perfect world that Byron's 'mysterious girl' inhabits. She seems to radiate from with, 'softly lighten[ed] o'er her face', 'the tints that glow', 'mellowed to that tender light'.

<u>Do you think the speaker is interested in speaking to this woman or is he happy to have her kept at a distance? Why?</u>

Light and darkness

It's an interesting study of subjectivity that this woman can only be seen in the context of light, and is completely defined by how she is shaded- 'one shade the more, one ray the less'. The night that she is compared to is itself defined by 'starry skies'. She is made purely aesthetic, purely a physical being, by the fact that she can

only be seen in light and has no obvious internal worth or complexity. Ironically, though she does not speak, her body speaks for her. Her cheeks or brow, in particular are described, somewhat improbably as 'eloquent', although the adjective could also be read as describing her smiles. Apparently her mind is also at peace [so basically there's nothing going on in her head] and her heart's 'love is innocent' [so she's never experienced any kind of relationship].

Alternatively, though she is defined by light, she can also be seen by it even when it is dark, like a beacon in 'the night / of cloudless climes'. She seems to have an inner radiance, generating her own light and this draws men to her, like a beacon. Or perhaps like moths to a flame. The fact that she remains removed throughout the poem suggests her inner light is like a lighthouse, warning ships away from a rocky shore. Is it possible that beneath the apparent serene beauty of this woman, hidden under the elegant and smooth poetic metre, and tucked inside the seemingly flattering imagery lurks something darker, dangerous and more threatening? The idea that a woman's beauty is dangerous is, of course, a common thread running through literature, but especially so at the time of the Romantic Movement. As Keats's *La Belle Dame Sans Merci* illustrates the vampire genre really took root by making female sexuality demonic and otherworldly. Can Byron's lady be read in the same way as some sort of femme fatale? Is the poem the dreamy expression of a bewitched potential victim?

This woman isn't blonde and beautiful, like an innocent child or angel. Rather she is dark [which brings into play the obvious negative connotations of 'darkness'] and 'of the night', a meaning which would have had much more impact on Byron's contemporary audience [particularly given his own liaisons with sex workers and other sexual encounters that would have been deemed immoral or illegal at the time]. Her hair is described as 'raven' black and ravens are, of course, associated with death and evil. Perhaps her description also implies innate sexual knowledge, her 'winning' smile luring the speaker [and the reader in] to her trust and affection.

In the end, though, this reading feels like forcing the poem into something it isn't. The significance of the various references to darkness in the poem is not due to connotations of evil or death, but rather that the lady is an ideal because in her the opposites of dark and light are perfectly reconciled. Yes, the poet is entranced by this figure and she does remain remote and rather ethereal. But there's nothing really convincing to suggest that her beauty and goodness is a trap luring in the besotted male.

What is certain in this poem is that the speaker uses the technique of synecdoche [using a part of something to describe the whole]. The only physical things we learn about the woman is a lot about her eyes, her face, and her dark hair, but the rest of her is presumably shrouded in the same darkness as the night which imposes as shade to make 'one ray the less'.

She Walks in Beauty crunched:

WALKS – BEAUTY – NIGHT – STARRY – DARK – BRIGHT – EYES – TENDER – HEAVEN – SHADE – RAY – GRACE – RAVEN – LIGHTENS – SERENELY – PURE – DEAR – ELOQUENT – SMILES – GOODNESS – PEACE – LOVE – INNOCENT

Christina Rossetti, *Remember*

Rossetti's poem, which opens 'Remember me when I am gone away', is oft-used at funerals. As such it has a cultural identity that aids its effectiveness in stirring sad emotions in us; joining other traditionally used elegies, it presents the speaker from beyond the grave as stoical, selfless and wise. Of course, the poem is spoken by someone living; yet the fact that it is most often used to give a voice to the dead means that it has taken on a different cultural legacy. Its immediate intelligibility lends itself to oral performance. We can hear it once and form a strong sense of its meaning. Rossetti uses very few obvious poetic flourishes or ornamentation; in keeping with the serious material and matter-of-fact tone, the language of **Remember** is unfussily modest and straightforward.

Rossetti was an English poet who belonged to a well-known group of artists and literary figures known as the Pre-Raphaelites. The Pre-Raphaelites sought to return to art as it was composed before or 'pre' the Italian artist Raphael. Specifically they wanted to revive the use of precise detail and intense colour pallets of 15th century Italian art. Christina Rossetti sat for some of the movement's well-known paintings, such as her brother Dante's *The Girlhood of Mary Virgin*.

Rossetti's most famous poem, *Goblin Market,* is full of dark and challenging subversions of the typical children's genre and has proved fertile ground for a host of theoretical excavations from feminists, psychoanalytical readers and Marxists. On the surface at least, *Remember* seems a less controversial, more conventional poem.

Remember x 4

The poem uses four 'remember's. The first two set up the command to remember, and the second two quantify these to re-iterate the need for the reader not to forget the speaker of the poem, the person who has died/ will soon die. The first two 'remember's are imperatives, setting the tone for the sentence that will ensue. So is the third; 'and afterwards remember, do not grieve'. However, the last one is in a subordinate clause, linguistically softer, less firm. It is as if Rossetti uses the four markers to take the reader through the journey of grief; from denial and anger in the first part of the poem, with firm, imperative language, to the sadness and acceptance of 'remember' being in the subordinate [or dependent clause].

The first two uses of the word also talk about the future, and the hope of what is lost; the 'silent land' of death is infinite, without the structure of the 'day by day'. Indeed the poem is full of ambiguous time frames- 'a while', 'our future that you plann'd', 'the thoughts that once I had'. Is it as if the speaker is already occupying that space where time has stopped working. The tone of the poem finds its home in a half-existence that is only conjured into being by the implied consciousness of the speaker. The second half of the poem distances itself even further from the present- 'yet if you should forget me for a while / and afterwards remember'. The poem takes us from the first, raw hurt of grief through to future healing in the space of a sonnet's fourteen lines- perhaps it is this swift, but restrained outline of the process of grief that leads people to be so emotionally affected by it.

Sometimes saying less, but saying less precisely, can mean more than using lots of looser words. Characteristically Rossetti uses euphemism to underplay the suffering involved in this scenario, including her own. She describes her death, for instance, twice with the casual, everyday phrase, 'gone away'. And death itself is described only as a 'silent land'. The grim reaper is banished from the poem. Absence of the beloved is imagined as no longer being able to hold their hand. The only moment when the chasm of grief begins to open up and threaten to crack the verse's marble-like surface is in the ominous phrase 'darkness and corruption'.

The poem's understated language may be composed predominantly of ordinary words, but their intense patterning is rhetorical. Repetition is a particularly marked feature. Anadipolis sounds like a long extinct dinosaur, but actually it's a term from rhetoric describing ending one line with a phrase and the using it at the start of the next line. Rossetti uses it with 'gone away / Gone far away'. Notice how the addition of the simple word 'far' adds emotional weight to the phrase. Other words and phrases repeated include 'no more', 'should', 'far', 'when' etc. Rhetoric, of course, is appropriate for a poem which seeks to persuade its reader of something. Rossetti's poem counsels the reader not to grieve. Subtextually, of course, it implies that they/ we must cherish the beloved while we can, before they leave us.

Naturally modern readers do not assume that male poets would be manly and resolute in attitude and matter-of-fact in style. Nor would we think men would especially demonstrate these qualities when facing a subject as grim as their own mortality. If we were tempted to make such gendered assumptions, many of the poems in this anthology would swiftly disabuse us. Equally, we would not expect female poets to be emotional in tone nor florid in expression. Nevertheless it is striking how Rossetti radically reverses Victorian gender stereotypes and it would be interesting to see whether students would gender the poem as male or female if the writer's sex was withheld. *Remember* might not subvert convention as obviously as *Goblin Market*, but it does, in this way, overturn Victorian expectations. Perhaps too the poem's firmly buttoned-up emotion, its stiff-upperlipness is also an essentially

 English characteristic. <u>Would the poem be more powerful if Rossetti released her emotions from all this restraint? Would we get something more American and, perhaps, something mawkish?</u>

Going down in good order

What's most striking about this poem is its control. Language is instrumentalised and employed with tremendous precision. There's not a touch of post-structuralist slipperiness to this language or any hint of what T.S. Eliot called the writer's 'intolerable wrestle with words'. Rossetti exerts mastery on her words and through them over her emotions. The management of structural aspects makes this most evident: syllables, the rhyme scheme, lineation, syntax and metre are all kept in good working order. For instance, each line is composed of exactly ten syllables, none are even one more or less. All the rhymes are also full and, despite the stringent technical challenges of the Petrarchan form with its limited number of rhyme sounds, the rhymes slide into place like parts of a well-oiled machine. Each of the first two quatrains is also composed of one sentence that completes itself neatly on the last word of each stanza. This repeated syntactical pattern also neatly brings the poem to the volta, after the octave, and the slight shift of focus in the sestet, signalled by 'yet'.

The metre too is a reliably regular iambic pentameter. Ticking over evenly, it keeps the underlying, potentially destabilising, emotions tucked away. Only on a couple of occasions can we hear small disturbances in the poem's even tread. Scan the lines and you'll notice only two slight deviations. The metrical wobbles occur in lines 3 and 12.

The first is a line composed entirely of monosyllables. A regular iambic pentameter would mean that the following syllables are emphasised:

'When **you** can **no** more **hold** me **by** the **hand**'.

Listen to the poem and the emphasis will, however, fall on 'more'. It's simply the more important word in the phrase 'no more' and the line invites a small pause before moving on to the verb 'hold'. Similarly 'me' is surely more important in terms of semantics than the preposition 'by' and thus takes more emphasis. The alliteration of 'm' sounds further foregrounds these two words. The tension here between the poem's metrical pattern and its semantic and sonic ones generates this ruffling in the otherwise smooth surface.

In the second example, the regular metre would be: 'A **vest**ige **of** the **thoughts** that **once** I **had'**, which would leave a clumsy and unnecessary stress on the small function word 'of'. Again, listen to the line and what we hear is more like 'A **vest**ige of the **thoughts** that **once** I **had'**. This is a technique known as pyrrhic substitution, where one stress is diminished, here 'of', so that the following one on 'thoughts' is strengthened. The metrical trailing off and then re-strengthening is highly appropriate to the sense of what is being said. Overall, the extraordinary control of the poem manifests over its material, the exertion of will and reason over destabilising emotions exemplifies, neatly, the poem's overt message to its reader.

<u>How, though, is the reader to feel about being accused, potentially, of forgetting this speaker</u>? Memory is a complicated thing because it calls into question what we call reality, and what we judge as being a real experience. The fact that this poem is culturally used most often to give voice to the dead [prosopopeia] as opposed to giving voice to those about to die means that there is a lack of ability for the reader to reply. Gently it may be, but the poem actually accuses the listener or reader of forgetting someone that they have lost- even the opening line wants to make the reader protest with something along the lines 'Of course I will!' The reader has no right of reply to these accusations, which means that they are left to examine and recognise their own shortcomings in relation to grief and moving on with their lives. There is a silence where there should be correspondence, or a counter-argument.

Because the reader has no opportunity to say that they will, of course, remember the person who has passed away, there is a double sadness to which people react:

the sadness of the death and the guilt that they might one day fulfil the accusation of the poem. Narrative silences are really important in literature because they indicate an inability to respond, and a conspicuous gap where there would otherwise be someone controlling the narrative. Interestingly, here it is the person who is either dead, or about to die, who has the voice; the person still living is made silent.

Do you think the poem would be more or less effective if it were a dialogue between two specified people?

Afterlife

The afterlife isn't exactly a bustling party here, or a vision of Bacchus handing out the wine on Mount Olympus. It's an euphemistically phrased 'silent land' which has none of the 'future that you plann'd'. Worse, as we've noted, it's full of 'darkness and corruption'. This is a living person describing the grave, not a voice describing heaven. It's interesting to point out that Rossetti rejected a fiancé because he turned back to the Catholic Church; she began to become interested in the Anglo-Catholic Oxford movement, becoming a woman of religious devotion. Five years before *Remember* was written [1862] she had had a religious crisis. It's striking, therefore, that death in this poem doesn't lead to resurrection in the life beyond. This could have been a point of consolation – I will be dead but will live on eternally in heaven – but this is not what Rossetti wishes to emphasise. Whilst the 'silent land' could at a stretch indicate the heaven of eternal rest [as put forth in the New Testament] it is a curious turn of phrase - to describe heaven as a sterile and 'dark' place is theologically dubious at best. It seems more likely that as a non-devotional poem, this work addresses the very real, frequent and everyday way of coping with the enormously high death rate in Victorian Britain. It has the tone of a didactic tale on how to cope with death.

There's an interesting dynamic in the fact that the speaker here effectively writes their own elegy. It's important to be aware of how we perceive control over a literary narrative- but even more here, the person about to die is trying to guide the memories that other people have of them, which form a sort of afterlife in themselves. It also creates and maintains the exact life after death which the speaker is arguing perhaps doesn't exist in the 'silent land'. Whenever the poem is read or spoken, this idea is continually recalled and comes to symbolise much bigger ideas of loss, grief and pain through Rossetti's unspecific and ambiguous terminology. She does not tie her speaker down to a time or a place; the lack of response from another voice means that the poem comes to represent all those who have passed away, and the slow transition of time that ensures an afterlife in memory, as well as a general fading of conscience.

Form and allusion

It's in the classic form of a Petrarchan sonnet, often used in poems where the subject is unrequited love. Normally, however, it is the speaker of the poem that is suffering from unrequited love; here it is the reader.

An allusion to the tale of Orpheus and Eurydice can be found in the line 'nor I half turn to go yet turning stay'. Orpheus, after the death of his beloved Eurydice, goes

down to Hades to ask for Eurydice back. Hades tells him that he can take her back to the living world on one condition; that on walking out of the Underworld, he should not look back at her, but instead carry on walking lest she be lost for ever. Obviously [because these things don't have happy endings] he turns around to see her because he lacks faith in what the gods have told him. The speaker of the poem wants the reader to have faith that they should be separated, and it is right and proper that this should happen; to chase the person who has died into the 'silent land', or Hades, is not what has been intended by fate. The same 'turning back' can also be found in the sestet, where the speaker describes 'Yet if you should forget me for a while / And afterwards remember, do not grieve'; it is implied that one turns back to grief as one turns back to a memory of a loved one.

Remember crunched:

REMEMBER – GONE – SILENT – HAND – STAY – REMEMBER – FUTURE – PRAY – FORGET – GRIEVE – DARKNESS – CORRUPTION – THOUGHTS – FORGET – SMILE – REMEMBER – SAD

Thomas Hardy, *The Ruined Maid*

So appalled was he by the critical reception of his latest novel, *Jude the Obscure* in 1894 that the novelist Thomas Hardy resolved to quit the form and turn instead to poetry. The novel's loss was poetry's gain. Though Hardy is famous for a series of great novels that stand alongside the work of Charles Dickens and George Eliot as the cream of Victorian Literature, he has also been as influential as a poet. Indeed a line from his work runs back and forward through the heart of English poetry. As we shall see, *The Runied Maid* highlights both sides of Hardy's literary skills, creating a vivid scene with dialogue, chararcter and costume and setting this within the frame of a regular poetic form.

Why were contemporary readers so horrified by *Jude*? You'll have to read this great, angry book to find out the full answer, but, basically it was because Hardy's novels confronted head-on some of the worst iniquities and most crippling hypocrises of Victorian society. His lowly protagonists struggle heroically under the crushing weight of a moralistic and judgemental, hypocritical and often immoral society. In particular Hardy's novels excoriate Victorian society for its hypocritical ideas about class and gender. Perhaps his most famous novel, *Tess of the D'Urbevilles*, for instance, is the story of a supposedly 'fallen' woman, outcast from society because a man forced himself upon her before she was married. But the novel carries a crucial secondary part of the title which reveals Hardy's own attitude: *A Pure Woman Faithfully Presented*. The poem before us follows a similar pattern, with the initial impression we might form developing into a reading more sympathetic to the plight of its emblematic female protagonist.

 It would be interesting to see if students are able to work out what has happened to this poem's 'fallen' woman. Try presenting the poem with the title and each use of the word 'ruined' redacted. The class's task would be to fill in the blanks. They might assume, perhaps, that different words are used in each stanza. Once you've discussed their findings consider the impact reading the title has on the way we read the poem and the cumulative impact of the repeated near-refrain featuring variations on the word 'ruin'.

All that glitters

From a casual reading it might initially appear that Hardy's poem is promoting prostitution as a rather good career opportunity for an attractive Victorian maid. The life of the titular maid appears to have been transformed for the better. Hardy makes a series of contrasts between her life before and after her ruination:

- Before she was tied to a village and to dull, back-breakingly hard physical, work such as 'digging potatoes, and spudding up docks'. Now she 'struts' freely around Town and says that she enjoys a life of idle leisure, she 'never' does 'work'.

- Moving from village to Town she has escaped life-destroying poverty and has found 'prosperity'.

- Her appearance has been transformed, both superficially and more profoundly. Before she was dressed 'in tatters, without shoes or socks'; now she wears pretty and expensive clothes, 'fair garments', 'gay bracelets', 'little gloves', 'bright feathers' and a 'fine sweeping gown'. Fair, gay, little [as in delicate] bright, fine, adjectives that could be applied to the woman as much as to her possessions. And, more fundamentally, her body has changed too: before her hands were crude, animalistic 'paws' and her face an unnatural 'blue and bleak'; now her good looks have 'bewitched' the other speaker and both her face and her cheek are described as being refined, as 'delicate'.

- Her language has grown more refined: where before she spoke with an accent, said 'thik oon' and 't'other', now she talks posh.

- Her demeanour and state-of-mind has been radically improved. Before she was deeply unhappy, she'd 'sigh' and 'sock' and called home-life 'hag-ridden'. At present, in contrast, now the maid agrees that she's 'pretty lively' now and is free of 'megrims or melancholy'.

Who in their right mind would choose to go back to the previous life?

Not our inquisitor, evidently, who concludes, understandably envious, 'I wish I had feathers...and could strut about Town'. As the list of advantages the change in the maid's life has secured pile up we may expect there to be some sort of sting in the tale. A final stanza perhaps where the true horror of working in the sex industry is brought suddenly, shockingly home to the complacent reader. But Hardy doesn't do this; why not? Isn't there a danger that, without something along these lines, the poem might be read as celebrating prostitution? Or why doesn't Hardy make a comment on the scene, like an intrusive narrator providing a moral frame to guide the reader?

To the first question, because it's not necessary. To the second, only for the stupid of grossly inattentive. To the third, isn't it more powerful if the implied moral condemnation is left to us, the readers? We already know from the outset, from the title, that the maid's life is 'ruined', an adjective that in Victorian culture would carry far more stigma. It has become her name, or her title, and the epithet sticks to the poor girl like tar throughout the poem. All these earthly trappings of apparent wellbeing disguise a much more fundamental corruption and exploitation, and, at some level, the ruined maid knows this. Hardy wants to be realistic too and to do so he must make prostitution sound like a potentially attractive option to a poor, young uneducated woman. Otherwise it might be all too tempting for us, at a safe distance from such harsh lives, to mount our moral high horses and condemn the young woman for selling herself into sexual slavery. Hardy's poem makes this distancing manoeuvre much harder; the poet makes us understand why individuals make such decisions; though the description of poverty is only sketched in, it is done vividly enough for us to appreciate the desperate drive to escape it. Understanding this, we should be more likely to sympathise with ruined maids. And, crucially, if the

individual is not to blame we then have to look at the system and the cultural values that allow or even encourage this sort of exploitation.

But, before we go on to that, let us consider how Hardy signals to the reader that the bright picture of the ruined maid's life is a sham. We have already commented on the repetition of the pejorative adjective 'ruined'. As well as appearing in the title, as if the woman's identity has now been subsumed by this phrase, it is also repeated at the end of each stanza. Everything in this poem comes back to the girl's ruination. Now, it's possible that her tone is arch, casual and sarcastic. Along the lines of 'they say I'm 'ruined' but look at what I've got!'. The maid could be brushing off society's hypocritical condemnation of her life by belittling and ridiculing the word 'ruined'. It's patently absurd to say her life's ruined, materially at least. And, of course, some readers might argue that women who work in the sex industry, then as now, could be seen as using their bodies willingly as commodities and that in some ways this could be viewed as empowering or, at least, shrewdly capitalistic. Hardy's poem, however, seems to be arguing the opposite. Even if we read the tone of the maid as being blithely insouciant, the way she keeps coming back to the word 'ruin' implies that at some, deeper level she feels this stain on her character.

Further evidence that the woman's apparent wellbeing is deceptive is the hedging verb 'seem' in the line 'you seem to know not'. As Hamlet commented, 'I know not seems'. Added to this, we have the obvious naivety of a narrator who speaks excitedly in exclamation marks and who is entirely seduced by appearances. Partly she acknowledges this seduction when she describes herself as 'bewitched'. Hardy's combination of novelistic and poetic skills really comes to the fore in aligning character to speech to metre to rhyme. Somehow he has to make the dialogue sound natural and to distinguish two speech patterns, so that both respective characters are brought vividly to life. Character and dialogue are, of course, integral to the novelist's art. At the same time he has to string the speech patterns across a technically very demanding metre, anapestic tetrameter:

'O **Mel**ia, my **dear**, this does **ev**erything **crown**!
Who **could** have sup**posed** I should **meet** you in **Town?**'

Anapestic metre has more unstressed than stressed beats; hence its lines skip along energetically. Even when there are slight variations the verse remains sprightly, onward moving. Hardy's choice of couplets enhances the effect – the first rhyme soon meets its partner and the verse moves swiftly on. Clearly this is not a metre/ rhyme pattern combination that would suit or prompt profound reflection. This lively, energetic, dance-like pattern fits perfectly the character of this speaker. Notably the metre remains restrained within the fixed, set and unchanging pattern of the stanza form. For, though these characters may appear to make choices and have agency of sorts, they operate within the locked and immovable wider pattern of the regular stanza form. An analogue, surely, for both individuals' relationship with wider society.

And whatever agency they do have is severely restricted. 'Melia says that she's *been* ruined, not that she's ruined herself. Hardy presents this as something that's happened *to* her, not necessarily something that she's had any real control over - again, a useful marker of his opinion on how society can be engineered to trap people into positions that they don't exactly wish for. 'Melia's lack of real agency contradicts her apparent increase in social mobility. Lastly, the poem's structure also contributes to the implied criticism. The narrator leads and controls this conversation; she sets the topic of each stanza, is the one that asks questions, makes observations, passes comments, speaks first and most. The ruined maid merely responds, subject to the other speaker's interests. She accepts and falls readily into this passive and reactive position, servicing another character's desires. The exception is, of course, the last stanza, where she has the last say- discrediting the farm girl's lack of knowledge, but ultimately still answering the question that is posed to her.

Social criticism

Another bitter irony for this poem is the contrast between the marketplace for virginity and the marketplace for sex. The amount of money that this girl can get for her sexual services seems to be more than the social worth she can get for her virginity. Hardy is criticising the difference between the physical vs. moral worth of one's sexual identity- just like he does in *Tess*.

A growing and influential body of thought in Victorian society argued that moral degradation could be recognised physically in 'criminal types'. Supposed 'physical stigmata' of criminality/ moral degradation included a sloping forehead and overlong arms.[9] As those features indicate, this thinking was influenced by Darwin's theory of evolution, with criminals considered to be evolutionary throwbacks. The maid's 'paw'-like hands might have been a similar 'stigmata'.Clearly and dangerously, Hardy contradicts the equation of beauty with goodness and ugliness with sin / criminality. The poem implies that not all finely dressed, middle or upper

---

[9]See, for example, the work of the Victorian criminologist Cesare Lombroso.

class people are necessarily moral. Appearances often are deceptive. Even fine ladies may be hiding something behind their appearances. Using irony, Hardy highlights the hypocrisy of a society that conceptualised poverty as immoral and potentially criminal, which would congratulate someone for lifting themselves out its maw, but then condemn them for how they did this, even when they played the only game available to them. Though this maid can pass herself off as a lady before a 'raw country girl', the poem makes it clear that polite society will quickly realise the truth and judge her accordingly. Her slip out of register in the final line betrays the strain of maintaining 'good'/ middle class impressions. 'You ain't ruined' is the sort of error that would give her away immediately and expose her to ridicule and disgrace. If there are prostitutes, there must too be their clients and the pimps and brothels and brothel-keepers to service that industry. As the girl's clothes indicate, a great deal of money was clearly being made through sexual exploitation of poor women whose lives in the process were 'ruined'. It is the heartless corruption of this form of capitalism that Hardy's poem protests powerfully against.

A Ruined Maid crushed:

TOWN – GARMENTS – RUINED – TATTERS – SPUDDING – BRACELETS – FEATHERS – RUINED – THIK – T'OTHER – POLISH – RUIN – PAWS – BLEAK – GLOVES – RUINED – HAG-RIDDEN – MELANCHOLY – RUINED – FEATHERS – FINE – DELICATE – RAW – COUNTRY – RUINED

Thomas Hardy, *At an Inn*

[If loving you is wrong] I don't want to be right

Thomas Hardy was never too keen on parties; didn't think much of standing on ceremony. But in May 1893 he agreed to put his head in at a gathering at the Viceregal Lodge in Dublin, the residence of the Lord Lieutenant of Ireland, and it was there that he first laid eyes on Florence Henniker. Florence, like Hardy, was a writer; and she, like Hardy, was married. She'd ankled down the aisle with Capt. Arthur Henry Henniker-Major in 1882, eight years after Hardy had taken the plunge with Emma Lavinia Gifford, whom he'd met while working as an architect on the restoration of St. Julitta's church in Cornwall. But Hardy and Emma had become estranged, and Arthur was away most of the time roughing people up in the Mahdist War. Florence and Hardy began a correspondence which, as time went on, suggested more than friendship between them.

The matter came to a head in the August of that same year when the fun-loving pair fixed up a day out in Winchester, the model for Wintonchester in *Tess of the d'Urbervilles* where [spoiler] the heroine gets executed. There may have been a touch of guided tour to it, because they walked up to the same spot where Angel Clare and Liza-Lu watch the black flag being raised to signal Tess's death, but the main event came when they turned up at the George Inn for a bit of sustenance and were wrongly assumed by the staff to be married. Hardy might have hoped that the misunderstanding would give them the jolt they needed, but it seemed to do the exact opposite. Neither romance nor sex were forthcoming, and, though the episode inspired *At An Inn*, their relationship was never the same again.

Greatest love of all

In a way it's understandable that the proprietors of the guest house assumed Hardy and Florence were man and wife. By this stage, after all, she was 38 and he was 53. Plus there's something pretty homely about a day trip to Winchester. What's more surprising is that, at least according to Hardy's account of the affair, they

immediately idolised and idealised the pair's relationship [which didn't even exist anyway]. Hardy describes their 'smiles' and how they 'warmed' on seeing the couple, their apparent 'zeal' in imagining the depth of their affection. He closes the second stanza with an imagined fragment

of their enthusiastic remarks – 'Ah, God, that bliss like theirs / Would flush our day!' – whose apostrophic appeal to God, coupled with 'bliss' and its connotations of heavenly joy, suggests an image of perfect, celestial love. Those overtones of divinity are strengthened by the reference to 'The spheres above', the vault of heaven, and the related 'love-light', which sounds like beams from those orbs of passion. With that beseeching exclamation mark at the end, too, which implies a loud and public voice, it reads like a bored spouse's prayer for romance and ideal love.

And there's a transformation of mere 'love' into 'Love' in the poem's third stanza, as 'love's dear ends' becomes 'Love's own pair'. The capitalisation seems intended to distinguish between regular human 'love' and a perfect 'Love' that has been blessed by God. This 'Love' is abstracted and idealised, somehow disconnected from worldly intimacy, and it seems that Florence and Hardy have [erroneously] been made the symbol of it: as 'Love's own pair' they are the emblems of love and, as 'pair' suggests, of marital bliss. This is, of course, not their own understanding: the significance is projected onto them by the innkeepers, whose enthusiasm in observation, whose vicarious pleasure, is captured in 'They warmed' and 'their zeal'. They're convinced: 'their thought' about 'what [TH + FH] were' is singular and definitive. As such, there's an unreality to it, not only because there isn't a romantic relationship between the couple, but also because no couple's relationship could be as perfect as the observers consider theirs. Hardy acknowledges this illusion with the repeated verb 'seemed / seem', with 'sport' and its connotations of theatrical performance, and with the image of the 'pane-fly' which redoubles that feeling of performance and examination by introducing a window to the scene, a window through which the couple may be watched and scrutinised, as in an observation room. Their relationship, which they are yet to recognise, let alone consummate, is turned into an illusory symbol of unrealistic love.

Feel like makin' love

Maybe it's because of the way their relationship is abstracted and fictionalised, or maybe it's because of the way he'd deluded himself about the whole thing. Maybe Winchester just put him in the mood. Whatever it was, Hardy seems fixated throughout the poem on the tangible validation of sex, and sexual imagery and sexual connotations pervade the poem – camouflaged, perhaps, but pretty unmistakable. There's the sense of bodies 'warmed' with pleasure, for example, the faces 'flushed' with the resulting rush of blood, and the 'bliss' of corporeal ecstasy. There's the description of 'living love' which, un-capitalised, suggests a more primal and basic form of intimacy, and whose present participle 'living' conveys action and energy and physicality. And then there's the description of the love 'which quicks the world' where 'quick' evokes the quickening of a heart beat and, with its connotations of life and vigour, reproduction and sex.

On the allusions and innuendo go. 'Bloom' can mean a flower, of course, but it can also mean the excited flush of a cheek. 'Sport' can stand for a play or entertainment, but can also refer to love-making. 'After-hours' indicates a bed, the symbol of sexual encounters, and has overtones of illicit, furtive activity, such as an extra-marital affair. 'Veiled' could suggest a nun or a bride, so either no sex or honeymoon sex but either way: sex. Even 'stand' can mean an erection, and used to be used more commonly in that context than it is today. 'Within his hold' rings of an embrace, and the two-become-one image of 'alone' ['all one'] smacks of sexual union. The spatial significance of 'between' in 'never the love-light shone / Between us there' evokes a desire for physical proximity and interaction. And the pointed repetition of 'come / came' in 'The kiss their zeal foretold, / And now deemed come, / Came not', particularly in the context of an unfulfilled 'kiss', seems designed to emphasise the word's well-known euphemistic meaning: orgasm. In short, *At An Inn* is littered with insinuations and double entendres, reflecting, perhaps, not only Hardy's desire to sleep with the woman he loves, but also to substantiate their relationship, to make flesh and blood what had been merely correspondence and speculation and fantasy.

Heaven's just a sin away

But this sexual union never came about, and that seems to be a] because Florence maybe wasn't actually that keen on Hardy, at least in that way, and b] because she just couldn't shake the feeling that sleeping with anyone who didn't happen to be Capt. A. H. Henniker-Major went against everything she stood for. Hardy writes of

the innkeepers' assumption that the couple 'had all resigned / For love's dear ends', but it seems that Flo just couldn't bring herself to resign those nuisance religious beliefs and conventional principles re. marital fidelity. Perhaps he sensed this might be a sticking point: he'd been going on at her to read Swinburne for ages, and had read Shelley's *Epipsychidion* with her in July, and both of the poets make a point of saying how 'love's dear ends' should take priority over the 'laws of men', or at least words to that effect. But the manacles of social propriety proved too strong, perhaps, and figures of religious / state / class repression lurk throughout the poem.

For example, all that stuff about their idealised, heavenly 'Love', the 'bliss' and the 'spheres', has a flip-side: the Church didn't think much of people going off for clandestine weekends to Winchester [or anywhere else] with someone who wasn't their spouse. Any loving and sex was to be done in 1. good faith, 2. the eyes of God. So that 'Veiled', with its connotations of a newly-wed's wedding garb, seems to haunt the poem as an emblem of unattainable honourable love, while the line 'Made them our ministers', where 'minister' means a priest, stresses how illegitimate their

 union would be with only an innkeeper as a pastor. Hardy can hardly escape the religious overtones: 'living love' recalls various similar constructions in the Bible, such as 'living Lord', 'living rock' and 'living waters'; 'quicks the world' echoes 'the quick and the dead';

'zeal' has connotations of religious fervour. The publicans may have thought their [imagined] love touched by the divine, but the Church and its doctrines are standing in the way of its consummation.

And it wasn't only religious dogma that was holding them back: there were also the customs and conventions of the upper classes to consider. Florence had an aristocratic background, but Hardy was a working-class boy from Dorchester who only moved in upper-class circles because of his literary fame. Originally he had moved to London to work as an architect, and had hated the city for its social divisions. It seems possible, therefore, that when Hardy writes of 'the living love / Which quicks the world – maybe / the spheres above', those higher spheres refer not only to heaven, but also to the aristocratic classes. It's at once a jibe – with the suggestion that love may not 'quick' the nobility – and a fearful acknowledgement that these people are watching over, ready to stamp out any improper behaviour. In the repetition of 'seemed / seem' there are echoes of 'seemly' and 'beseeming' – respectable conduct – and terms of judgement and condemnation proliferate: 'deemed', 'cast', and 'stand' for standing trial.

Hardy refers to the couple's 'port', their safe harbour, their secure world of love within the world, but this sanctum is disrupted by the 'laws of men', the social orthodoxies maintained by the upper classes. The several half-rhymes – 'care / were', 'sympathy / maybe', 'ministers / theirs' – manifest this tension, while the stanza-structure, which sees each pair of lines formed by the splitting of one line of iambic pentameter, communicates how [at least, to Hardy's mind; see part a] above] the pair have been forced apart. Unable to consolidate their relationship, made powerless by the repressive forces of Church and society, their love is paralysed, or 'palsied', and left to die.

What becomes of the broken-hearted

So nothing happens: no sex and no romance. They end up just two middle-aged people in marriages that didn't satisfy them, looking for a bit of excitement, unable to take the final step. When they got on the train back from Winchester, it wasn't just the end of the excursion, it was the end of any lingering possibility for love. Hardy must have known it was over when he wrote *At an Inn*, and an undeniable fatalism touches the poem, most obviously in that phrase 'palsied unto death', but elsewhere too. There's the sense of 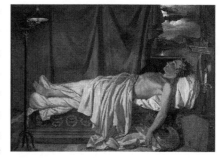 conclusion and finality in the line 'love's dear ends', for example, and the connotations of the death-bed in 'chilled the breath'. 'Resigned' could stand for 'given up hope'. The emphasis on the adjective, reinforced by the alliteration, conveys the feeling that, though the 'love' may have been 'living' once, it isn't anymore. 'Veiled' recalled a wedding veil, but it could just as soon be a funeral one.

There's a certain weariness, the sense of a man feeling his age. He acknowledges that the 'bloom', with its overtones of freshness and youth, were 'not [theirs]'. Time hangs heavy on the poem, with repeated references to 'days' and the 'spheres above' which govern the passing of months and years. The allusions to the 'afternoon' and 'after-hours' are in the same category, but have the additional significance of often being used to refer to middle-age, later life, the decline towards death. Love may 'quick' the world – but in doing so it hastens it towards death. When Hardy begs to 'stand' once more as he and Florence 'stood then', it isn't merely out of desire for another shot at the affair, but is also, as Proust would say, in pursuit of lost time.

At an Inn... crunched:

STRANGERS – CARE – VEILED – THOUGHT – WARMED – OPINED – RESIGNED – ENDS – SWIFT – LIVING – QUICKS – SPHERES – MINISTERS – GOD – BLISS – FLUSH – ALONE – LOVE – LOVE-LIGHT – BETWEEN – CHILLED – AFTERNOON – PALSIED – DEATH – ZEAL – COME – NUMB – PORT – BLOOM – SPORT – AFTER-HOURS – SEEMED – DAY – SEVERING – LAWS – DEATH

John Keats, *La Belle Dame sans Merci*

Scholars seem to agree that the Romantic poet, John Keats, had a rather problematic attitude towards women. Though he was attracted to young women, he was also repelled by what he considered to be their flirtatious and untrustworthy behaviour. In particular, the poet had a long, difficult relationship with his beloved, Fanny Brawne. Keats's letters show that he often worried about whether Fanny Brawne really loved him and that he was jealous of any attention she received from other men. Simultaneously he fretted about being trapped in their relationship:

'Ask yourself my love whether you are not very cruel to have so entrammelled me, so destroyed my freedom'.

And love itself, he sometimes described in his letters as an affliction: 'A man in love I do think cuts the sorryest figure in the world'.

Though, as we will see, this poem can be read in many ways, and although not all its mysteries can be neatly resolved, at its simplest level, dressed in medieval garb, supernaturalied and mythologised, featuring a character entrammelled and imprisoned, **La Belle Dame Sans Merci** expresses Keats's ambivalent feelings about the power of love, sex and women.

A few years before completing *La Belle Dame* Keats had written in *Edymonion* that 'A thing of beauty is a joy forever', one that will 'keep a bower quiet for us, and a sleep / full of sweet dreams'. His *Ode to a Grecian Urn* concludes with the resounding declaration that 'beauty is truth, truth beauty' and Keats's poetry, as a whole, can be seen as a quest after beauty. But *La Belle Dame Sans Merci* upsets his equation of beauty with truth: Certainly the titular character is beautiful, but the knight is mistaken when he thinks she loves him 'true'. Rather than bringing him peace, the knight is left the sorriest figure, 'haggard and woebegone', 'alone and palely loitering'. Beauty in this poem is entrancing, captivating, but it is also deceptive, dangerous, draining. Perhaps this is why, simultaneously some sort of goddess and demon, the figure of La Belle Dame cast such a powerful spell on Keats's imagination.

A safe distance

Keats's ballad features two narrators - a frame narrator who begins the poem and asks questions, and a knight who takes up the narration in the fourth stanza. Mysteriously the frame narrator disappears from the scene, diminishing to only a faint linguistic echo in the last stanza, leaving a lingering sense of incompleteness to the poem. This begs the question, <u>what is the function of the frame narrator and why does he, or she, vanish</u>? Firstly, the narrator twice asks questions of the knight; what is wrong with him and why he is wandering about like a lost soul. Use of the apostrophe, 'O', implies concern for the knight, indicating that the narrator is not merely an objective or disinterested observer - somehow they are emotionally involved in the poem's events. As well as setting the scene and witnessing the knight's anguished state, the narrator also seeks an explanation for the pale knight's strange, wandering behaviour.

The literal minded among us may wonder what exactly the narrator was doing near this silent, withered lake, where he [or she] happens upon the 'haggard' knight.

121

Perhaps Keats is suggesting that the narrator is potentially another victim of La Belle Dame Sans Merci, somebody who has also strayed from the safety of civilisation and from the masculine sphere of action. Just as the knight is warned by the dead men, so the knight warns the narrator. The narrator seeks answers from the knight perhaps so that [s]he can avoid meeting the same apparently cruel fate. If we accept this reading, Keats uses the narrator to amplify the story, to suggest that there is something universal in the pattern of seduced and betrayed men. Unwarned, the narrator might have followed the knight who has, in his turn, followed the 'pale warriors' to the elfin grot. Initially it is as if the narrator is asking us their questions, which places us, albeit momentarily, in the position of the knight. Hence the poem implies the reader too can be drawn into its seductive narrative.

There is another way of looking at this. As we've said, on one level Keats's poem is about the dangers of falling in love with a beautiful, but untrustworthy woman and dramatises his fear that women may betray men. At the heart of the poem there appears a pretty straightforward story of a short-lived love affair followed by a break-up. However, Keats wishes to explore and understand his feelings by getting some perspective on them, examining them from a distance. Hence he supernaturalises and medievalises the story, transforming it into a timeless myth. The use of the two narrators reflects the way in which the poet tries to distance himself from his experience, adopting the seemingly safe position of frame narrator as well as of the armoured and armed figure of a knight. The fact that he slips so seamlessly from outside observer to protagonist suggests the power of the story to dissolve such defensive strategies, to draw Keats in. Similarly, the knight's armour offers him no protection against the bewitching Belle Dame.

The knight

The transition from narrator to character could have been indicated through the use of speech marks. Keats employs these to indicate the speech of the woman and the dead men too. So why not use them when the knight speaks? If the poet had wanted to distinguish clearly between the two speakers he could also have given them different language, in terms of register, vocabulary and rhythms. Taken together, it seems that Keats wished to deliberately blur any distinction between the two characters. They are either two potential victims, or essentially two versions of the same person, one before and the other after encountering La Belle Dame.

Obviously the knight fits with the Romantic medieval atmosphere of the poem. The medieval setting also implies that this is an archetypal story, a timeless pattern of behaviour repeated eternally. This would all be true if the character were a wandering minstrel, or such like. A 'knight', however, has connotations of an ideal man: nobility of character, masculine strength and power, action, heroism, the highest standards of chivalry etc. In medieval Romances knights fight and vanquish monsters in order to win the hand of beautiful, virtuous maidens. In Keats's twist of the story, the beautiful, virtuous maiden turns out to be the monster. And if a knight and other noble characters, such as kings and princes, can be so easily undone what chance for ordinary mortals? Or, indeed, poets?

The effect La Belle Dame has on the knight is specific:
1. He loses blood and looks ill; he is exhausted, enfeebled and feels 'forlorn': 'O what can ail thee'...'fever'...'palely'...'haggard'...'woebegone'.
2. He is isolated ['alone'] and stripped of his active, heroic role - he is away from battle, aimlessly 'loitering'. He has become the wandering ghost of his former self. Once a man of noble action, all he can do now is to pass on his dreadful warning.
3. Moreover, his appearance suggests that the knight has been emasculated. Both similes in the third stanza use flowers associated with feminine beauty, the lily and the rose. The process of his loss of male power, a symbolic castration, can be traced through the verbs used in the middle section of the poem. On first meeting La Belle Dame, the knight appears to be in control. He is the active subject of the verbs 'I met', 'I made', 'I set'. These three little, simple monosyllabic verbs, coming at the

start of three successive stanzas, summarise a swift, bold courtship. The gallant knight sweeps the lady off her feet and onto the back of his horse. Like Caesar, he came he saw and he swiftly conquered. All the lady does is make a 'sweet moan' and 'sing'. Easily won, she seems very compliant.

Before becoming entrapped by La Belle Dame the knight makes her presents, love tokens of a 'garland' and a 'bracelet' and, despite her saying nothing, he confidently reads her looks as showing 'she did love'. Perhaps the elision of 'if' in this line is ominous; the knight suppresses any doubts he might have. There's also a subtly disturbing, ambiguous quality to 'and sure in language strange she said'. If the language is 'strange', or foreign, how can he be 'sure' of what she is really saying? And we often use 'surely' to express doubt, not certainty.

The sixth stanza begins the reversal in power. Agency of the verbs switches to La Belle Dame. The knight becomes their passive object. He is lulled into being the submissive partner:

- 'she found me'
- 'she took me'
- 'she lulled me'

Fed and 'lulled' to sleep, he is further unmanned and diminished by being infantilised. Only in his unquiet dream does he escape the enchantment. Even here he is a passive witness rather than active agent. Significantly, Keats uses the same verb to forge a link between the knight and the narrator. Both see pale victims of La Belle Dame, both are warned of her seductive, but treacherous beauty.

Imagination, in the form of a dream, warns the knight of his fate as another victim of the mysterious enchantress. When he wakes the 'elfin grot' has disappeared and he is alone on a hill. What would you do in this situation? Run as fast as your legs would take you, back to battle and the manly world of knights, I warrant. <u>Warned, why then doesn't this knight escape?</u> For one thing he seems to have lost his 'pacing steed' and is now on foot. Clearly this symbolises a loss of status and masculine power. Though he appears to be alive, he also seems trapped by his experience, doomed to repeat it as a story. Or perhaps he's so pale and haggard, so withered because now this knight is now just a ghost, unable to leave the place where he lost his life.

La Belle Dame

Unless, rather perversely, we take the narrator to be female, the poem is told entirely from a male perspective. Notably, La Belle Dame Sans Merci never has the chance to express her opinions, or to explain her motivation. Her voice is silenced.

<u>Who, or what, is this beautiful 'faery' woman?</u>

We know some key things about her appearance: she's 'full beautiful', with 'long' hair and 'wild' eyes. Keats emphasises this last feature through repetition of the same adjective in stanza eight, 'her wild, wild eyes'. Conventionally eyes, of course, are considered windows to the soul. So she's uncivilised and unpredictable in some essential way. Objectified and evaluated, the woman is characterised only through the vague generalities of her physical attractiveness and her untamed otherness. We learn that she's also exotic, non-human, supernatural in some way; 'a faery's child' she lives in an 'elfin grot'. Her home is away from towns and people, somewhere in the wild ['the meads']. Her appearance suggests a lost damsel from a Romance story. Initially she's docile and virtually mute, just making 'sweet' moans, and she seems extraordinarily easily wooed. All it takes is a few 'garlands' and she's off on the knight's horse; hardly the behaviour of a civilised lady of virtue. Her virtual silence and easy compliance with the knight's wishes seem to make her more attractive to him. From his male perspective she's the perfect fantasy woman. The knight hardly has to do anything to persuade this beautiful woman to leap into his arms.

Peculiarly, when she gets the knight home to her 'grot' she just cries and 'sigh'd full sore'. How are we to read this weeping? Regret at what she is going to do? Regret that, like the knight, she is trapped in this narrative pattern? Or are her tears meant to signal her duplicity? Vulnerability a subtle weapon to make the knight lower his guard even further?

Sweet tooth

After seeming entirely submissive at first, suddenly La Belle Dame takes control. She feeds the knight, as if fattening him up with tasty, exotic, heavenly food -'relish sweet', 'honey wild' and 'manna dew'. The food can also have another symbolic

significance. According to the critic, Lionel Trilling, 'for Keats, the luxury of food is connected with, and in a sense gives place to, the luxury of sexuality'. In other words, eating fruit is coded reference to sexual intercourse. If we accept this, then the poem dramatizes Keats's fear that love and intercourse might lead to some sort of entrapment and loss of male power. And in this reading, the lady behaves with a liberty that would have been deeply shocking to a polite nineteenth century audience.

Then she sends him to sleep, presumably through some form of enchantment [though he already seemed bewitched]. Here she takes on the role of a mother, feeding and putting a child to bed. Does this make La Belle Dame more disconcerting? A fairy lover, demon, goddess, enchantress, inverted mother/ witch figure? Probably yes.

The phrase 'in thrall' signals that she has made the knight her slave or servant, diminishing him even further. We also learn that many men have been victims and that she has a name: La Belle Dame Sans Merci. <u>Can we presume she must be French?</u> Either the whole poem is set in France [but the characters fortunately speak English] or else she is French and foreign to the knight. Perhaps this adds to her impression of exotic otherness. Written not longer after England had been at War with France, La Belle Dame's Frenchness might also make her seem a more threatening or symbolic figure, more of which anon. Clearly the repetition of the adjective 'pale', used about both the knight and the other 'pale...death-pale' victims, indicates that they have lost blood. In this sense La Belle Dame seems to be some sort of Gothic blood-sucker, a vampire, perhaps; beautiful, predatory, deadly. That would fit with her hard-to-categorise, or liminal, quality. Or she could just be an exotic beautiful woman, one whose 'wild'ness indicates that she has rejected nineteenth century society and its rigid constraints on female behaviour. In either case, she remains a fictional version of Fanny Brawne.

Unmasking La Belle Dame

Read metaphorically, however, she could be a personification of death, or disease. Bringing 'fever' and 'anguish', weakness and 'paleness', she leaves her victim listless and forlorn [and perhaps also dead!]. Arguably she is a symbol for the irresistible power of tuberculosis, the disease that killed Keats and several members of his immediate family. Some critics have also suggested she could symbolise drug addiction; we know that at one point during his illness Keats's friends were appalled to find he had been dosing himself with laudanum.

More radically still she could be read as a symbol of imagination, beauty or even of poetry itself. The manly knight falls in love with the woman and turns a melancholy, emasculated poet! Alas! Certainly Keats sometimes worried that imaginative adventure, the intoxication of poetry, might be a way of avoiding engaging properly and actively with the real world. In this interpretation La Belle Dame is the goddess muse of poetry who enchants and enslaves the will of the male poet.

Or if we go back to her Frenchness, La Belle Dame could symbolise the revolutionary ideas that drove the French Revolution. Many of the Romantic poets were captivated by these ideas and some championed the cause of revolution - Wordsworth and Blake were notable enthusiasts. However, the aftermath of the revolution was bloody and chaotic, as one form of tyranny was replaced by another just as virulent. During the 'Reign of Terror' thousands of people were publically executed and hopes for a better, fairer, more just society were swept away by a rising tide of blood-letting.

All these readings are plausible. The great thing with symbols is they're polysemic – they can pack in many meanings inside one image – and still retain their mystery. It is part of what makes Keats's poem so captivating.

Dead men talking

As with the narrator, the dead men amplify and universalise the story of the individual knight, suggesting he is one in a long line of victims stretching into the future, unless warned by other noble men. The Gothic grotesque description of their suffering, with 'starved lips in the gloam' with horrid warning gaped wide' is also disturbing, warping the fairy tale frame of the story, making it darker and more sinister. These Gothic elements accord, of course, with the vampire reading.

A poetic spell

Keats's poem doesn't just describe an enchantment; it weaves its own spell on the reader. How does Keats' generate the poem's hypnotic effect? Mainly through setting, repetition, adaptation of the ballad form and the poem's overall structure.

The setting is sketched in a few quick strokes:

'The sedge has wither'd from the lake
and no birds sing'

A tense and eerie atmosphere is conjured by the silence and we may wonder why no birds are singing - a notorious sign of danger. The verb, 'withered' suggests decay and links the landscape to the knight on whose cheek a 'fading rose/ fast withereth too'. Keats uses pathetic fallacy here so that the landscape seems to reflect the knight's mood and mindset. As with the narrator and other dead men, this device suggests more is at stake than the fate of a single knight.

With one exception, the conjunction 'and' is used in every stanza. Sentences are organised in a simple narrative fashion: This happened and then this happened and then this happened. The absence of subordinating conjunctions indicates that Keats does not explain the events, just sets them out before us, so that they retain their mystery. The gently insistent repetition of diction, syntax, and metre establishes the poem's incantatory rhythm. The pulse is also muted - there are few emphatically stressed syllables. The repetition of the muted rhythm further enhances the trance like feel. Each stanza ends with a full stop and follows the same pattern. Hence,

though the story moves onwards, there is a counter force of stillness and stasis.

Keats also adapts the ballad metre. Conventionally a ballad is written in quatrains of alternating four beat [tetrameters] and three beats [trimeters] often in iambic feet. Keats stretches the second lines into tetrameter: 'Alone and palely loitering'; 'So haggard and so woebegone'; 'With anguish moist and fever dew'.

Ti-TUM ti-TUM ti-TUM ti-TUM

And he docks a beat from the fourth lines. Look, for example, at 'and no birds sing', 'and made sweet moan', 'on the cold hill's side', which all end heavily with three stressed monosyllables in a row. At other times the poet trims the last line of the quatrain back further: 'with kisses four', 'hath thee in thrall', 'a faery's song' are dimeters – just two beats. The unbalancing, stretching and cutting of the form creates tension at the end of each stanza, a feeling of being brought up short, or something being not quite right or as expected. Another way of thinking of the metre is in terms of rising and falling. Traditionally the second line has the falling quality of a trimeter following a tetrameter. By lengthening this line Keats has three lines with a rising quality, hence accentuating the dying fall of the final line of each stanza.

Overall the poem has a cyclical structure, with the last stanza's language echoing the first two. This link between the start and end highlights the interesting passage of time in the poem. The first two stanzas and the final one are in the present tense, 'ail', 'loitering', whereas the story the knight tells is in the past tense, 'I met', 'her hair was'. It is almost as if after the knight has told his story we re-enter the same moment, as he answers the narrator's question.

Working together the various aspects conjure a feeling of suspended animation, of time stuck, held and halted, which further strengthens the poem's hypnotic, haunting spell.

La Belle crunched

KNIGHT-AT-ARMS – ALONE – WITHER'D – NO – AIL – WOEBEGONE – FULL – DONE – LILY – FEVER – FADING – WITHERETH – LADY – FAERY'S – HAIR – EYES – GARLAND – FRAGRANT – LOVE – MOAN – STEED – NOTHING – SING – FAERY'S – RELISH – MANNA – STRANGE – TRUE – ELFIN – WEPT – WILD – KISSES – LULLED – WOE – DREAM'D – COLD – PRINCES – DEATH-PALE – BELLE – THRALL – STARVED – WARNING – AWOKE – HILL – SOJOURN – ALONE – WITHER'D – SING

NB
Perhaps we have overstated one reading; that the knight has been trapped and possibly even killed by the La Belle Dame. Another possibility is that he is so pale and feverish because he feels guilt at what has happened in the 'elfin grot'. Perhaps La Belle Dame is more innocent that we'd supposed, perhaps she is even the victim.

Differences are often as revealing as similarities. Comparing Keats's poem to Willian Blake's *The Garden of Love* highlights stylistic features of both poems. For example, adjectives are very significant in *La Bell Dame sans Merci*; they establish mood and atmosphsere and carry essential meaning. Keats uses alot of them. In the first two stanxas, for example, he uses four to describe one subject, the knight:'alone and palely loitering', 'haggard' and 'woe-begone'. Other important, repeated, adjectives include 'cold', 'wild', 'pale'and 'sweet'. In comparison, predominantly simple monosyllables, the verbs in Keats' poem are mostly functional and colourless. The density of adjectives contrasts with the scarcity of verbs and in particular dynamic verbs which convey action. This imbalance is another contributor to the feeling of supsended animation.

As with Keats's poem, the verbs in *The Garden of Love* tend to be functional, mostly anglo-saxon monosyablles that fade into the background on reading. Take the first stanza which features the dull verb 'went', as well as 'saw', seen', 'was' and 'used to play'. However Blake uses far fewer adjectives than Keats and when he does use them they are more functional. The only adjective in the first stanza is the informative 'built' and there's a similar adjectival phrase, 'in the midst'. The simple verbs, the lack of vivid adjectives and adverbs combined withsimple conjunctions throw stronger emphasis on the captitalised nouns, 'Garden of Love', 'Chapel'. Blake's language is thus more stripped back, leaner and starker.

Blake developed relief engraving, whereby the background of a copper plate was cut away so that the design was left standing out from the metal, the opposite of conventional engraving technique. Look at any of Blake's designs and you'll notice the importance of strong, thick lines, almost like in cartoons. Probably his aesthetic was shaped by his love of Gothic art and through his training as an engraver. The stark, bold design of *The Garden of Love* certainly shares a similar aesthetic, where the most important things, the key nouns, stand out markedly from the background words.

Hostile critics have sometimes accused Keats of rather enjoying languishing in his melancholy, arguing that he is a bit too willing to be imprisoned in the sensuous 'bower' or 'elfin grot' he has created. Sometimes his fondness for adjectives is criticised as excessive; such larding of the arteries of his verse, it is argued, creates an unmanly floridity. Another poet who seems to rather savour his melancholy and another poet haunted by a beloved is our last one, Ernest Dowson.

Ernest Dowson, *No Sum Qualia Eram*

For sentimental reasons

If it's possible to be more infamous than famous then Ernest Dowson is more infamous than famous. His infamy is due in part to people like the contemporary poet, Arthur Symons, saying things like, 'Without a certain sordidness in his surroundings he was never quite comfortable, never quite himself,' and going on about his terrible drinking / predilection for prostitutes / so forth. And it's due in part to his paedophilic infatuation with a Polish girl called Adelaide 'Missie' Foltinowicz, owner of the world's sassiest nickname and eleven-year-old child [when E.D. first met her], who was, understandably, very adverse to the idea and ended up marrying a tailor. But Dowson, the massive creep / old romantic, found it pretty hard to move on, and the sentimental ache which pervades lots of his poetry is often put down to the loss of this Adelaide.

Non sum qualis..., whose 'Cynara!' is often read as an Adelaide-cipher, is up there with his very most sentimental, one of the works which crowns him as the Victorians' undisputed king of yearning. 'Last night, ah, yesternight...,' for starters, has to be top ten most wistful openings to anything ever: the speaker only gets two words in before he heaves this big, nostalgic sigh, 'ah', which you think for a moment might be, 'aye', as in, 'yes', as in, 'Last night, yes, yesternight', but which you realise is, yes, just a heavy, transcribed exhalation of longing. Plus poems or songs re. 'Last night' or 'Last summer' or 'Yesterday' have a tendency to be pretty wistful [see: Paul McCartney]. Dowson's opening is particularly so because a] it reiterates the 'Last night' sentiment within the first four words ['Last night' / 'yesternight'], and b] 'yesternight' was, by 1891, when this poem first appeared, already quite archaic. It's as if Dowson is trying to talk his way back into the past, or haul the past into the present, or both.

As if to confirm that this effect is no accident, there's another of those current / archaic pairs in the poem's first stanza – viz. 'betwixt' and 'between' – emphasising the speaker's commingling of past and present. This commingling finds its grammatical embodiment in the present perfect verb tense, the hybrid construction where the past and the present coexist, of the refrain's 'I have been faithful.' This construction reappears in more expansive form in the poem's third stanza, which begins, 'I have forgot much, Cynara!' Subsequent clauses, 'gone with the wind,' and 'Flung roses, roses riotously with the throng,' are qualified by the 'have' of 'I have forgot much' to become present perfect rather than just simple past. And this poem-long past / present liaison reaches its climax in the final, one-sentence stanza. It begins with simple past ['I cried for madder music'], flirts with present perfect ['But when the feast is finished'], and finally embraces the unadulterated present of this melancholy speaker:

'Then falls thy shadow
the night is thine
And I am desolate'.

Shadows and fog

This conflation and confusion of past and present has a wider consequence: it seems linked to the motif of Presence / Absence which runs through *Non sum qualis...* and touches almost every aspect. When, for example, the speaker finally seizes on the present tense in 'Then falls thy shadow, Cynara!' the phrase an almost-exact repetition of a past-tense counterpart, 'There fell thy shadow, Cynara!' Moreover, the phrase concerns a 'shadow', a form which is both There [in that it is visible and cast by some substantial body] and Not There [in that it is transient, contingent, and by definition an absence of light]. If this is Cynara's shadow, then she must be there; and yet we know she isn't. For not only is the speaker's yearning never sated, and not only is each appeal to 'Cynara!' embellished with an exclamation mark which recalls the figure of apostrophe [the invocation of some absent person / thing], but also the shadow is not literal; instead it is a haunting figment of the mind which the speaker can't expel.

Shadows and a dearth of colour are metaphors which surface often in Dowson's poetry, evoking a dismal, greying world in which bright colours are only seen fleetingly. The 'bright red mouth' of the poem's second stanza, for instance, soon fades to the 'grey' of the 'dawn,' just as 'lilies' are wont to 'pale'. This monochromatism appears to have been a preoccupation for the poet who wrote of his generation's best novelists that they 'must squeeze the colour from his brush, and dip it into the grey pigments,' and whom Arthur Symons said could be made to find no pleasure in the iridescence of the ballet: 'I could never get him to see that charm in harmonious and coloured movement, like bright shadows seen through the floating gauze of the music.'

Dowson's palette, coupled with the gloomy Christian connotation of 'shadow' [namely, 'Valley of the Shadow of Death'], communicates the same profound cheerlessness captured in the resigned 'I was / am desolate' of the poem's refrain. And yet 'desolate' has a meaning beyond 'forlorn', one which informs the Presence / Absence theme: 'Desolate' can also mean 'solitary' or 'alone' or even 'uninhabited'. What's interesting is that, when the speaker says 'I was desolate' the first couple of

135

times, he does so as part of the description of a scene in which he is lying in bed with a woman ['bought red mouth' suggests she's a prostitute]. As such, he is identifying himself as simultaneously in company and in solitude. The implication of this paradox is clear: no company except Cynara's could ever remedy his loneliness, and though this [presumed] prostitute is resoundingly corporeal and tactile and there, evoked synecdochically by 'lips' and 'heart' and 'mouth', we understand that she will provide the speaker no lasting relief.

Comfortably numb

There seems, therefore, to be a divorce between the speaker's mind and body: he is both accompanied and alone, both present and removed. That he is at once, in this way, both conscious and unconscious of his surroundings is reflected in an [presumably deliberate] inconsistency in the second stanza: the speaker says that 'All night' he felt the beating of the woman's heart, and is aware of her lying in his arms 'Night-long', which both imply he didn't sleep; and yet he says, 'When I awoke'. The man is both alert and sleeping. His mind is elsewhere; his body 'uninhabited', as 'desolate' suggests. It isn't clear whether he is engaged with empirical sensations or not, for when he says, 'Surely the kisses of her bought red mouth were sweet,' that 'Surely' might well mean 'truly' [i.e. 'certainly'], but equally it might mean 'in all likelihood...' or 'common sense suggests...' or 'I assume [though can't be sure]...' It's as if his absent mind hadn't really registered what his body had experienced.

And while it seems the speaker is numbed to the 'real' sensations of the external world – the 'music' which is not mad enough; the 'wine' which is not strong enough; the 'dawn' which is not bright enough; the woman who is not Cynara – there is, at the same time, an obsession with 'seeing' which isn't really seeing, with imagined, 'visible' forms which seem more real to the speaker than the real world around him. There are, of course, the shadows which inhabit the poem [and, moreover, unreal shadows: shadows which are cast after 'the lamps expire'], but there are others, too. There are the 'lilies' of the 'mind', unambiguously abstracted, poetic symbols of Cynara. And there are 'the lips' of the speaker's 'desire', the physical / visible embodiment of his abstract longing.

Read my lips

But lips symbolise more than just physical attraction and sexuality. They are also associated with speaking and the voice, and this relates the image to another incarnation of the Presence / Absence motif in *Non sum qualis...* For, though I have been referring throughout to 'the speaker', there is really no speaker in the poem [unless someone reads it aloud, and even then we'd never say that they have become the 'speaker']. Yet we regularly resort to metaphors of a voice when speaking about poetry, and seemingly can't help but 'hear' one as we read. The poetic voice, as such, is spectral, both present and absent [like Cynara / the lilies / the prostitute / the protagonist], lurking behind the page but disappearing as soon as we try to look at it directly. This paradox, this complication of text and voice, became a point of great interest and excitement for Victorian poets, and Dowson was no exception.

That nostalgic 'ah' in the poem's first line, for example, is unmistakably an attempt to transpose into writing a primarily vocal phenomenon, to record the operations of lungs and throat and mouth and tongue in printed characters. And this transposition to a more permanent medium is at once successful [for we recognise it as a sigh], and doomed, because the life that made the voice a voice is lost. It's like a butterfly on a pin. Then follows the description of Cynara's 'breath', a word with connotations of both life and voice, which isn't exhaled, as we might expect, but 'shed', like tears or blood. Not only, therefore, does 'shed' ascribe a physicality to the breath which more often we associate with text, but also, in conjunction with 'wine' and 'passion', which end the next two lines, recalls the Crucifixion and communion [shed blood / altar wine / The Passion], where everything is both one thing and another: Christ is both man and God; bread is both grain and flesh.

So perhaps, to Dowson, the written word embalms the voice: it's preserved and honoured, but it's still dead. And yet, besides the 'ah', there are moments in *Non sum qualis...* where you sense a voice attempting to emerge from the text, to re-animate itself. The most obvious examples are those when the protagonist cries out, 'Cynara!' There's the apostrophe angle here, of course, but exclamation marks are also interesting because they are the most conspicuous means by which a writer can try to capture a particular tone of voice in writing; even to imbue the writing with a particular 'tone of voice'. For, while exclamation marks can affect the meaning of a sentence, more than questions marks, commas, full-stops, semi-colons or whatever, they are used for modulations of sound, rather than modulations of sense.

Or, at least, that might usually be the case. But in the hands of Dowson, those commas, full-stops, semi-colons etc. are also tools for adjusting the pace and intonation and sound of the verse, as much as fine-tuning its semantics. This is particularly true of the first published version of *Non sum qualis...* in which the punctuation is much more dense than in subsequent editions. Take the second stanza, for example. In that original, 1891 version it read:

'All night, upon my breast, I felt her warm heart beat;

Night long, within mine arms, in love and sleep she lay:

Surely the kisses of her bought, red mouth were sweet?

But I was desolate, and sick of an old passion,

When I awoke, and found, the dawn was gray:

    I have been faithful to thee, Cynara! in my fashion.'

So thick is the punctuation here, especially with the commas, that the meaning actually becomes more ambiguous; the semantics are put under strain. Meanwhile, however, those elements which we might more associate with a voice [speed, articulation] are pretty precisely dictated, as if there is, after all [though these sounds will forever be but imitated and imagined], a single voice present in the poem.

But this semantic strain and ambiguity seems not merely intended to foreground the verse's sound and vocal elements, but also to be a thematic concern. For the loss of the ideal moment, the fading, ecstatic memory, is a central subject of *Non sum qualis...* with its shadows, its interweaving tenses, its present / absent heroine and protagonist and voice. As the memory of the loved one dwindles, as the pursuit of the past become ever more desperate and less fruitful, the coherence of the self in the present becomes less certain. After all, as the title, itself recycled from the Roman poet Horace, acknowledges: 'I am not what I once was.' In the final lines, the speaker says, 'I am hungry for the lips of my desire,' and there's the slow revelation that, more than any real girl Cynara might have been, this man, this ageing man who's 'sick of' his 'old passion', is 'hungry for ... desire,' hungry for the youthful appetite which once he had and now has lost.

Non sum qualis... crunched:

AH – YESTERNIGHT – SHADOW – KISSES – SICK – DESOLATE – FAITHFUL – CYNARA – HEART – ARMS – RED – GREY – FORGOT – ROSES – PALE – LOST – MUSIC – EXPIRE – NIGHT – DESIRE

With its central theme of being haunted by an absent or impossible love Dowson's poem could be compared to many others in the anthology. *The Flea* and *To his Coy Mistress*, for instance, also explore barriers to love, or perhaps lust. Blake's *The Garden of Love* and Wyatt's *Whoso List to Hunt* face different sorts of barriers, while *She Walks in Beauty* and *La Belle Dame sans Merci* feature characters also entranced and perhaps bewitched by beautiful women.

NB

If, perchance, you're wondering about the source of the rather striking illustrations accompanying this essay, such as the one above, a couple are the works of the Victorian artist Audrey Beardsley. Beardsley produced the covers and interior designs to **The Yellow Book**, a journal of the aesthetic movement of the 1890s, to which Dowson also contributed material.

A sonnet of revision activities

1. Reverse millionaire: 10,000 points if students can guess the poem just from one word from it. You can vary the difficulty as much as you like. For example, 'yesternight', would be fairly easily identifiable as from Dowson's poem, whereas 'alters' would be more difficult. 1000 points if students can name the poem from a single phrase or image – How about 'amorous birds of prey'? 100 points for a single line. 10 points for recognising the poem from a stanza. Play individually or in teams.

2. Research the poet. Find one sentence about them that you think sheds light on their poem in the anthology. Compare with your classmates.

3. Write a cento based on one or more of the poems. A cento is a poem constructed from lines from other poems. Difficult, creative, but also fun, perhaps.

4. Read 3 or 4 other poems by one of the poets. Write a pastiche. See if classmates can recognise the poet you're imitating.

5. Write the introduction for a critical guide on the poems aimed at next year's yr. 12 class.

6. Practice comparing and contrasting: Write the name of each poem on a separate card. Turn face down and mix up the cards. Turn back over any three cards at random. What do two of the poems have in common? How is the third one different? Replace the cards and do the exercise again.

7. Use the poet Glynn Maxwell's typology of poems to arrange the poems into different groups. In his excellent book, *On Poetry*, Maxwell suggests poems have four dominant aspects, which he calls solar, lunar, musical and visual. A

solar poem hits home, is immediately striking. A lunar poem, by contrast, is more mysterious and might not give up its meanings so easily. Ideally a lunar poem will haunt your imagination. Written mainly for the ear, a musical poem focuses on the sounds of language, rather than the meanings. Think of Lewis Carroll's *Jabberwocky*. A visual poem is self-conscious about how it looks to the eye. Concrete poems are the ultimate visual poems. According to Maxwell the very best poems are strong in each dimension. Try applying this test to each poem. Which ones come out on top?

8. Maxwell also recommends conceptualising the context in which the words of the poem are created or spoken. Which poems would suit being read around a camp fire? Which would be better declaimed from the top of a tall building? Which might you imagine on a stage? Which ones are more like conversation overheard? Which are the easiest and which the most difficult to place?

9. Mr. Maxwell is a fund of interesting ideas. He suggests all poems dramatise a battle between the forces of whiteness and blackness, nothingness and somethingness, sound and silence, life and death. In each poem what is the dynamic between whiteness and blackness? Which appears to have the upperhand?

10. Maxwell argues too that the whiteness is a different thing for different poems. Consider each poem's whiteness in the light of this idea. See any differences?

11. Still thinking in terms of evaluation, consider the winnowing effect of time. Which of these poems do you think might be still read in another 200, 500 or 2000 years? Why?

12. Give yourself only the first and last line of one of the poems. Without peeking at the original, try to fill in the middle. Easy level: write in prose.

Expert level: attempt verse.

13. According to Russian Formalist critics poetry performs a 'controlled explosion on ordinary language'. What evidence can you find in this selection of controlled linguistic detonations?

14. A famous musician once said that though he wasn't the best at playing all the notes, nobody played the silences better. In Japanese garden water features the sound of a water drop is designed to make us notice the silence around it. Try reading one of the poems in the light of these comments, focusing on the use of white space, caesuras, punctuation – all the devices that create the silence on which the noise of the poem rests.

15. In *Notes on the Art of Poetry*, Dylan Thomas wrote that 'the best craftsmanship always leaves holes and gaps in the works of the poem so that something that is not in the poem can creep, crawl, flash or thunder in'. Examine a poem in the light of this comment, looking for its holes and gaps. If you discover these, what 'creeps', 'crawls' or 'flashes' in to fill them?

16. Different types of poems conceive the purpose of poetry differently. Broadly speaking Augustan poets of the eighteenth century aimed to impress their readers with the wit of their ideas and the elegance of the expression. In contrast, Romantic poets wished to move their readers' hearts. Characteristically Victorian poets aimed to teach the readers some kind of moral principle or example. Self-involved, avant-garde Modernists weren't overly bothered about finding, never mind pleasing, a general audience. What impact do the *Love Through the Ages* poems seek to have? Do they seek to amuse, appeal to the heart, teach us something? Are they like soliloquies – the overheard inner workings of thinking – or more like speeches or mini-plays? Try placing each poem somewhere on the following continuums. Then create a few continuums of your own. As ever, comparison with your classmates will prove illuminating.

Emotional..intellectual

Feelings..ideas

Internal..external

Contemplative..rhetorical

Open..guarded

NB

Yes, we know. This is that rare old bird, a sixteen-line sonnet, following the example of the poet George Meredith, no less.

Critical soundbites

In this demanding revision activity, students have to match the following excerpts from criticism to the poet whose work they describe. [Answers are at the end of this book]. In an added twist for this second volume, some of the soundbites come from the poets themselves...

1. 'A strand of recent criticism brings out a perceived protofeminism in the sexual politics of his poetry where it is interpreted as rejecting enslavement by sexual power.'

2. 'The persona's desire for the reluctant Lady is mingled with revulsion at the prospect of mortality and fleshly decay, and he manifests an ambivalence toward sexual love that is pervasive in his poetry.'

3. 'He created an immensely popular Romantic hero—defiant, melancholy, haunted by secret guilt—for which, to many, he seemed the model. He is also a Romantic paradox: a leader of the era's poetic revolution, he named Alexander Pope as his master; a worshiper of the ideal, he never lost touch with reality.'

4. 'In the opening lines the seducer assumes a pose of disdainful insouciance with his extravagant parody of the Petrarchan blason.'

5. 'Sexual energy is not an inherent "evil," but the repression of that energy is. The preachers of morality fail to understand that God is in all things, including the sexual nature of men and women.'

6. 'Many of his poems develop a single theme. Statements of feeling are tight-lipped and masculine, not overstated or ironised.'

7. 'The brilliance of his word play, his spinning out of startling analogies and conceits, find at work deliberate intelligence, no imagination; a talent of the surface, not of the depths, for which dalliance with language is more erotic than dalliance with the beloved. He moves by surprise than truth.'

8. 'He is often called a pre-Romantic poet for his sensitivity to nature, his high valuation of feeling and emotion, his spontaneity, his fierce stance for freedom and against authority, his individualism, and his antiquarian interest in old songs and legends.'

9. 'A pale imitation of the metaphysical Donne, echoing the earlier poet's assured, lithe rhetoric as well as his manly posturing, but lacking his predecessor's ironic wit and wry self-awareness.'

10. 'Nor did he seem by nature to be cheerful: much of the criticism around his work concerns its existentially bleak outlook, and, especially during his own time, sexual themes.'

11. 'The inconstancy of human love, the vanity of earthly pleasures, renunciation, individual unworthiness, and the perfection of divine love are recurring themes in their poetry.'

12. 'A yearning for a past love ebbs and flows dreamily under the influence of the 12-syllable French line.'

13. 'He forged a modern style that nonetheless hewed closely to poetic convention and tradition. Innovative in his use of stanza and voice, his poetry, like his fiction, is characterized by a pervasive fatalism.'

14. 'Characteristically, this quest for a transcendent truth can be expressed [or even conceived of] only in the terms of an intense, imaginative engagement with sensuous beauty.'

15. 'Literature for him was more than a dreamy refuge for a lonely orphan: it was a domain for energetic exploration, "realms of gold," as he later wrote, tempting not only as a realm of idealistic romance but also of a beauty that enlarges our imaginative sympathies.'

16. 'There is a marked class anxiety, as the speaker seeks to define his role, whether as a friend, a tutor, a counselor, an employee, or a sexual rival.'

Glossary

ALLITERATION – the repetition of consonants at the start of neighbouring words in a line

ANAPAEST - a three beat pattern of syllables, unstress, unstress, stress. E.g. 'on the moon', 'to the coast', 'anapaest'

ANTITHESIS - the use of balanced opposites

APOSTROPHE – a figure of speech addressing a person, object or idea

ASSONANCE – vowel rhyme, e.g. sod and block

BLANK VERSE – unrhymed lines of iambic pentameter

BLAZON – a male lover describing the parts of his beloved

CADENCE – the rise of fall of sounds in a line of poetry

CAESURA – a distinct break in a poetic line, usually marked by punctuation

COMPLAINT – a type of love poem concerned with loss and mourning

CONCEIT – an extended metaphor

CONSONANCE – rhyme based on consonants only, e.g. book and back

COUPLET – a two line stanza, conventionally rhyming

DACTYL – the reverse pattern to the anapaest; stress, unstress, unstress. E.g. 'Strong as a'

DRAMATIC MONOLOGUE – a poem written in the voice of a distinct character

ELEGY – a poem in mourning for someone dead

END-RHYME – rhyming words at the end of a line

END-STOPPED – the opposite of enjambment; i.e. when the sentence and the poetic line stop at the same point

ENJAMBMENT – where sentences run over the end of lines and stanzas

FIGURATIVE LANGUAGE – language that is not literal, but employs figures of speech, such as metaphor, simile and personification

FEMININE RHYME – a rhyme that ends with an unstressed syllable or unstressed syllables.

FREE VERSE – poetry without metre or a regular, set form

GOTHIC – a style of literature characterised by psychological horror, dark deeds and uncanny events

HEROIC COUPLETS – pairs of rhymed lines in iambic pentameter

HYPERBOLE – extreme exaggeration

IAMBIC – a metrical pattern of a weak followed by a strong stress, ti-TUM, like a heart beat

IMAGERY – the umbrella term for description in poetry. Sensory imagery refers to descriptions that appeal to sight, sound and so forth; figurative imagery refers to the use of devices such as metaphor, simile and personification

JUXTAPOSITION – two things placed together to create a strong contrast

LYRIC – an emotional, personal poem usually with a first person speaker

MASCULINE RHYME – an end rhyme on a strong syllable

METAPHOR – an implicit comparison in which one thing is said to be another

METAPHYSICAL – a type of poetry characterised by wit and extended metaphors

METRE – the regular pattern organising sound and rhythm in a poem

MOTIF – a repeated image or pattern of language, often carrying thematic significance

OCTET OR OCTAVE – the opening eight lines of a sonnet

ONOMATOPOEIA – bang, crash, wallop

PENTAMETER – a poetic line consisting of five beats

PERSONIFICATION – giving human characteristics to inanimate things

PLOSIVE – a type of alliteration using 'p' and 'b' sounds

QUATRAIN – a four-line stanza

REFRAIN – a line or lines repeated like a chorus

ROMANTIC – A type of poetry characterised by a love of nature, by strong emotion and heightened tone

SESTET – the last six lines in a sonnet

SIMILE – an explicit comparison of two different things

SONNET – a form of poetry with fourteen lines and a variety of possible set rhyme patterns

SPONDEE – two strong stresses together in a line of poetry

STANZA – the technical name for a verse

SYMBOL – something that stands in for something else. Often a concrete representation of an idea.

SYNTAX – the word order in a sentence. doesn't Without sense English syntax make. Syntax is crucial to sense: For example, though it uses all the same words, 'the man eats the fish' is not the same as 'the fish eats the man'

TERCET – a three-line stanza

TETRAMETER – a line of poetry consisting of four beats

TROCHEE – the opposite of an iamb; stress, unstress, strong, weak.

VILLANELLE – a complex interlocking verse form in which lines are recycled

VOLTA – the 'turn' in a sonnet from the octave to the sestet

Recommended reading

General books on writing, reading & analysing poetry:

Atherton, C. & Green, A. Teaching English Literature 16-19. NATE, 2013

Bowen et al. The Art of Poetry, vols.1-3. Peripeteia Press, 2015

Brinton, I. Contemporary Poetry. CUP, 2009

Eagleton, T. How to Read a Poem. Wiley & Sons, 2006

Fry, S. The Ode Less Travelled. Arrow, 2007

Heaney, S. The Government of the Tongue. Farrar, Straus & Giroux, 1976

Herbert, W. & Hollis, M. Strong Words. Bloodaxe, 2000

Meally, M. & Bowen, N. The Art of Writing English Literature Essays, Peripeteia Press, 2014

Maxwell, G. On Poetry. Oberon Masters, 2012

Padel, R. 52 Ways of Looking at a Poem. Vintage, 2004

Padel, R. The Poem and the Journey. Vintage, 2008

Paulin, T. The Secret Life of Poems. Faber & Faber, 2011

Schmidt, M. Lives of the Poets, Weidenfield & Nicholson, 1998

Wolosky, S. The Art of Poetry: How to Read a Poem. OUP, 2008.

About the authors

Head of English and freelance writer, Neil Bowen is the author of many articles and resources for a range of publishers. Neil has a Masters Degree in Literature & Education from Cambridge University and he is a member of Ofqual's experts panel for English. He is the author of *The Art of Writing English Essays for GCSE*, co-author of *The Art of Writing English Essays for A-level and Beyond* and of *The Art of Poetry*, *volumes 1-5*. Neil also runs the peripeteia project bridging the gap between A-level and degree level English courses: www.peripeteia.webs.com

James Browning was awarded a double first degree in English Literature by the University of Cambridge. His particular interest at uni. was 20th century Anglo-American poetry and he wrote dissertations on the New York School poet, Frank O'Hara, on Dylan Thomas, and T. S. Eliot. He is currently a private tutor and is working on his writing.

Johanna Harrison studied English Literature at Regent's Park College, Oxford University, writing her dissertation on Benjamin Britten's post-war opera libretti. She is now a professional opera singer and also runs a summer programme in the arts and humanities.

Head of A-level English, Michael Meally, holds an MA in American Literature as well as degrees in English Literature and Engineering. Michael's literary interests include detective/crime fiction, postcolonial literature and Greek tragedy. He is the co-author of *The Art of Writing English Literature Essays for A-level and Beyond* and *The Art of Poetry, vols. 1, 3, 4 & 5*. Michael writes regularly for the English & Media Centre magazine.

Answers to critical soundbites:

1. Wilmot, *suprisingly*
2. Marvell, *obviously*
3. Byron, *heroically*
4. Marvell, *repeatedly*
5. Blake, *erotically*
6. Wyatt, *manfully*
7. Donne, *wittily*
8. Burns, *Scottishly*
9. Lovelace, *critically*
10. Hardy, *glumly*
11. Rossetti, *stoically*
12. Dowson, *wistfully*
13. Hardy, *novelistically*
14. Keats, *aesthetically*
15. Keats, *once againly*
16. Shakespeare, *inevitably.*

You will have noticed we threw in the curve ball of extra soundbites for some of the poets. But can you tell which one of these comments is a work of fiction? A final revision task: Students either research or create their own anonymised critical soundbites; the class have to match the soundbite to the poet/ poem.

Critical soundbites adapted from:
http://www.poetryfoundation.org
Schmidt, *Lives of the Poets*
The Guardian online